It's No Puzzle

A memoir in artifact

Cris Mazza

Spuyten Duyvil
New York City

Acknowledgements made to the following publications in which these essays first appeared: Full Bleed for "Complex List." Diagram for "Ask the Depot Commander." The Rupture for "Camera: A Life Story." The Los Angeles Review for "June: The Mother We Thought We Knew." Tupelo Quarterly for "Someone Said No." The Los Angeles Review of Books for "Getting Their Stories Straight." Diagram for "We're Still Waiting." Trnsfr for "Yearbook Matchmaker."

With most of the books I've written, I was anxious for my parents to get to know me through stories and words. Now I wish they could see the pages where I'm trying to get a little closer to knowing them.

Thanks must go to Diane Goodman who read these essays in draft and assured me someone would care. To the University of Illinois at Chicago College of Liberal Arts & Sciences for helping me with the tools and time for archiving and writing. To all my siblings for our shared and traded memories. To my sister, Lee, who scanned and studied our mother's yearbooks for me. And to our parents.

ISBN 978-1-956005-65-3

We can't resist this rifling around in the past, sifting the untrustworthy evidence, linking stray names and questionable dates and anecdotes together, hanging onto threads, insisting on being joined to dead people and therefore to life.

Alice Munro
The View from Castle Rock

IT'S NO
pu ZZ le
MaZZa
A.S.B. TREAS.

This aimless story of poster-making didn't organically scream to be a part of any of the essays in this volume, and yet the poster rose to the status of the book's title.

My single foray into public service was running for student council office at the end of 7th grade. Knowing I wasn't popular enough to be president, nor even vice president, and didn't have the handwriting skills for secretary (an office always held by a girl in this era, and its gendered function didn't appeal to me for that reason either). Treasurer, then. I wish I had an image of the frenzied disorder I made of the ASB budget book.

But for my campaign, my slogan was proposed, and the posters designed by my mother. This survivor was one of from a dozen to twenty identical posters crafted on differently colored paper. A film fragment of memory suggests it was a group project with one of my sisters assisting as well. By 7th grade I must have had the scissor-skills to cut out the letters after we traced them from stencils on coarse black construction paper. The light ruler-lines, to ensure the two Zs were pasted level and centered but also to regulate the handwritten letters, are visible. But the puzzle of the puzzle-poster is who wrote the handwritten parts. The "pu" and "le" of puzzle could be me. But the curvy R suggests another writer. Yet I like to assume (and recall does suggest) my mother would have had me make the handwritten finishing touches myself.

In "June: The Mother We Thought We Knew," I've referenced an elementary school classmate who, much later in life, told me she'd "always pictured my childhood home as one where the mom was regularly organizing crafts, games and activities." An understandable assumption considering my mother was our Girl Scout leader. This poster is, at least, evidence of some validity in that girl's whimsical view. And that view is somehow part of everything else.

Complex List

where things are, where things go, and how it feels to know

After November 2016 happened to us, I wrote: *Two weeks in, have we all started, and abandoned, an essay about how this feels?* Then it was abandoned.

Before November 2016 happened to us, congestive heart failure completed its run, ending my mother's 16 months of hospice. In Spring of 2016, while the world was likewise occupied crafting digital memes for more pressing concerns, I filled hours of absorbed concentration (and a compartmentalized avoidance of grief) making a slideshow of her life. It started with the earliest black-and-white snapshots, Mom as an infant, 1925 or '26, lifted from the brittle black pages of my grandmother's photo albums; then my mother's own B&W snapshots, in an equally fragile album, high school and college years in Boston and moving west in 1946 to her first job teaching P.E. at a boarding school in Southern California. Then I moved on to scan her many thousands of color slides beginning in 1950, taken before she went back to snapshots in 1982, and to digital in 2005. Swimming, skiing, archery, field hockey, sailing, hiking, camping, lifeguarding; and after meeting my father she embraced fishing, hunting, gardening, concocting feasts, raising children, creating parties, leading girl scouts, more camping and hiking; driving the interstates to visit zoos, theme parks, museums, monuments both natural and manmade; after retirement she visited Europe, Canada, Mexico, Alaska, Panama, on trains and huge cruise ships plus one small tour vessel that she watched sink after evacuating to a rescue boat, bemoaning that her camera was on the floundering ship so she couldn't take photos of it going down (she saved the news clippings instead). Her life was a month short of 91 years, her lifetime photo collection numbered over five thousand. The slide show was 25 minutes, 275 photos. It was the weeks of hours of putting it together that made it seem I could hold the whole of her life in a comprehensible and continuing entity.

Then when November 2016 happened to us, I needed a new method to recede, to let my brain imagine living in another era and elsewhere, to muffle the fear and calm the agitation of ubiquitous news reporting. I became immersed in a genealogy project, working with some distant cousins I'd never met and whose political alliances I didn't know and didn't ask. Like a biologist narrowing the known world down to the illuminated circle at the end of a microscope, my deliberation was the size of my monitor's blue-lit square. Documents from ship manifests, marriage listings, censuses— 1890, 1900, 1910, 1920, 1930—gave me three great-aunts all named Maria with occupations called *typewriter*, *dressmaker*, *embroidery*, referring to the worker and not the machines being operated. Their Italian middle-names mutated from Elizabetta to Eliza, Grazia to Grace, Raffaella to Anne to Mary; and their mother Fortunata was born with the same Mazza surname as her husband. Never getting off my ass, I found two Mazza heads-of-household per each street address—along with wives, sisters-in-law, children, nieces, nephews—whose employment developed from *grocery* to *metal shop* to *jewelry*; WWI draft cards that lied about a dependent mother who had died 2 years prior; a sister marrying her deceased sister's husband who was also 1st cousin to both; names disappearing from Brooklyn and showing up in New Jersey at another crowded multi-family house. *Lives* being moved, morphed, maneuvered, maintained, managed, between 1895 and 1935. Lives already lived. In reverie: re-dramatized, re-traveled, re-invented, re-invigorated … instead of doing the same to my own.

When January 2017 started to happen to us, my canine partner in training, in dog event competitions, in life, consumed two searing weeks with a chaos of illnesses and my failed attempt to thwart a final decision. I couldn't save him, but I saved the evidence of him: In some cases whole folders from my file cabinet—health records, kennel club registries—moved intact into a plastic envelope and into his archive box, in other cases separate acid-free letter-sized envelopes organized: His paper pedigree and dog-magazine articles about accomplishments amassed by the litter he was part of; score sheets from memorable wins that I no longer specifically remember; genetic clearances for his hips, heart and eyes before he began his standout career as a stud dog, and the contracts with those who bred to him; his AKC title certificates and programs from the national championship performance events he attended; his puppy collar, last adult collar, baby teeth, swatches of his longest fur, a piece of white window blind he chewed in panic when I moved and left him alone in a new house; five sympathy cards, one from the vet whose care was largely a long list of medications that helped kill him; and a certificate inviting him to Westminster that arrived a month after he was gone.

> # CONGRATULATIONS
>
> OTCH High Times Wild Turkey UDX14 OGM SH
>
> has qualified to pre-enter
>
> ## Westminster 2017
> ### 2nd Annual Masters Obedience Championship

His 11x17" box then lifted to the top shelf of the closet that already holds the blue shawl worn by my great grandmother when she got married in the lighthouse where her father was keeper; fishing lures from the 1930s and 40s, which my father actually used, now antiques; a hand-embroidered tablecloth made by my mother and given to her mother for Christmas almost 75 years ago; and many other boxes of family archives detailed later in this essayed list.

At some point I noticed, numbly, with little surprise or indignation, that I'd lost sensation in erogenous zones. Meanwhile I filled a folder with loose slips of paper, each containing a scrawled memory exemplifying his personality, with intention to someday put each into a single exquisite sentence. But I never did. Instead I lost myself in 1946, the occupation of Germany and my father's assignment there overseeing the radio corps; the transmission of the Nuremberg trials to the U.S.; a train depot where war and manufacturing materials were being gathered and redistributed; and a group of German POWs housed in the depot whose rations were meager, who were not allowed to have radios, but who planned and invited my father to poetry readings. Through my father's paper archives and artifacts, and questions he was having difficulty answering, I built a story he never told, beside an overview of American policies in the German occupation. The concerns and resulting decisions of General Eisenhower, and the never-quite-averted retaliation plan to starve Germany, both rattled and strangely assuaged my avoiding-2017 self (there were *always* shitheads!). But mostly the work cocooned me successfully through 2017 into 2018, except that my father died three days before the final essay was ready to be published.

While 2018 was happening to us, almost exactly in the middle, there was a week of can't-be-grasped-unless-you've-done-it, face-to-face stare-downs with existential nihilism: clearing out Mom & Dad's residence of 50+ years. Which made it also my childhood home. The WiFi and sole TV already disconnected, no better way to remain insulated from the looming end of democracy, apparently as hopelessly chaotic as the collapse of my beloved dog's body. In contrast, our father passed easily with a few mumbled words, possibly to our mother, a final exhalation, a horse-drawn trip into a military cemetery, the clear cry of a bugle playing taps. The trauma and demise of his household over the week that followed: ten times the tumult. Then my little station wagon headed east, loaded with material for narratives that might never be written because, mercifully, I was also loaded, to the car's capacity, with more material for the family archives. Besides a few hardbacks from an earlier era of book reading (with Mom's bookplate: 1938 illustrated *The Story of Mankind* and 1931 *Leaves of Grass*; Dad's bookplate in the 1944 boxed set of Shakespeare, even though that year he was in the Army anxious to get over to Europe before "it" ended), I packed: approximately a thousand loose snapshots stripped from 40-50 post-slides / pre-digital photo albums (leaving 5 times that many still entombed in the plastic pages); my share of Mom's watercolor paintings and her snapshot record of *all* her (hundreds of) paintings; a portfolio of Dad's military papers—every single military order, some still in triplicate, requests and approvals for leave, instructions for storing and wearing officers' uniforms, receipts for military issue, mess cards that instructed *Retain This Card* (so he did … for 70 years)—which I'd organized the year before but he'd never looked at. Plus unexpected bounty: from 1946 Berlin artifacts to a never-opened tube of

educational posters about nuclear fission circa 1950; from letters my parents had written to each other (Mom planning their children's names a month after the wedding) to Dad's college composition essays upon his return to school on the G.I. Bill. with titles like "Youth of Today" (topic was juvenile delinquency) and "Can He Express Himself Freely?" (first amendment) and "The Guard" (about the unit of Polish Guard under his command in 1946 Nuremburg).

As 2018 dragged us to its last days, I finished archiving the treasures gleaned from the family compound, including scanning the 1000+ snapshots and organizing them by date, then systematizing the snapshots of every watercolor my mother had produced (not by date but by subject-matter). So when 2019 began happening to us, I went back to those 30+ years of slides, and not only began to methodically scan the rest of them, but I wanted them returned to their elemental order, by date and numerically in original film-batches. Through the 60s and 70s, Mom had acquired dozens of Airequipt slide magazines and began making slide shows by subject instead of by each roll of film, most notably each of her five children in childhood. Many other slide magazines did stay in date-oriented sets—excursions, vacations, holidays. Then in the 90s, she decided she

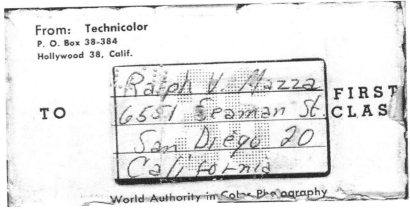

would take apart *all* the old slide magazines and make slide carousels for each of her children—i.e. divide all of the thousands of slides among us, assessing for each slide which of us would value that image the most. This project was unintentionally terminated when only two carousels of 80 slides each were completed. The rest of the slides were either loose and loosely organized by our names in old cassette-tape boxes, were still in a slide-magazine (almost half of them) or still in boxes from photo labs (almost another half, and not always the original box, dates and subjects crossed out and new ones written over). I liberated every slide from its magazine or carousel or box, appropriated my dining-room table plus a few auxiliary tables, and worked for months: sorting slides by year, then sorting each year by separate dated rolls of film. All the while I was also scanning, labeling each scan with the year first in the jpeg's name, organizing the scanned jpegs into folders by "era" (where the family lived) or subject (like *camp*). After every slide was in order in its original film batch—raising some arresting imaginary stories of film-disasters such as when a roll of film for a trip to Maine had all of 4 surviving slides—I inserted each into a plastic archive slide sheet, 20 slides per sheet; then 20 to 22 sheets in each slide-sheet binder, seven such binders in all. The first two-thirds of my parents' life together, from 1950 through the early 80s, stacked itself on my computer, and in plastic pages, and in my imagination: Their wedding and honeymoon, their early residences and omnipresent gardens, their budding family—first and second babies warrant many dozens of photos at 2 months then again at 3, 4,

5 months; rolling over, sitting up, sucking on toys and fruit and drumsticks, dressed in starched ruffles and bonnets or denim overalls or not dressed at all. Then as more children came along, events start to amass: our birthday

parties and Halloween costumes, our Easter finery and Christmas bikes, our first (and many after) hooked trout, our first (and many after) hikes in the Sierras; best friends, cousins, grandparents, family dogs, pet roosters and butterflies, litters of white bunnies soon to be dinner but for now bouncing on the lawn; snowball fights, sandcastles, riding the surf on canvass rafts, running naked in sprinklers; The San Diego Zoo starting in 1953, Knott's Berry Farm starting in 1955, Disneyland starting in 1958,

and the now defunct Santa's Village also 1958; finger-painting, science fair projects, musical instruments, scout uniforms, batting stances, patio cookouts; countless harvests of voluminous fruits, vegetables, flowers and eggs; equally innumerable hunting yields of duck, dove, quail, geese, and rabbit; girl and boy scout campouts, Christmas festivities, marching band, first cars and first formals, graduations; driving trips across the country, I-40 attractions and East Coast beaches, Washington D.C., Boston, Maine, Niagara Falls, Yellowstone. And threaded between every event or milestone or accomplishment or scenic excursion, the continued evolution of their last house, our family compound; built on the side of a hill and, over the course of 50 years, terraced with hand-constructed walls of rock dug out of the same ground by one man, assisted by his wife and children.

While 2019 was happening to us, to some of us more than others, I was given the benefit of a research assistant—a PhD student exiled from teaching by the college due to threats of concocted (bad) publicity from a troubled and bitter undergraduate.

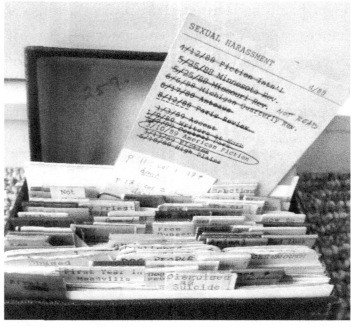

Together, on the floor of my campus office, my RA and I amassed and began to organize the boxes of archived papers that had been collecting for over four decades—going back to high school material. Not only the manuscripts—many versions of each novel and short story in hard copy from the first 2/3 of my career, pre-digital through semi-digital when submissions still had to be hard copy—but also the submission records for each on both 3x5 cards and an overall handwritten log; published versions of stories, essays and excerpts in literary magazines and anthologies, roughly 250, sliced out with an Exacto knife by my research assistant; letters from publishers, agents and editors, including acceptance letters and contracts for the fore-mentioned lit mags and anthologies. Then alone, in my 2019 summer job, I went through four document boxes containing every review and piece of publicity for each title; every other random piece of correspondence, from a N.Y. editor who unofficially agented and advised for a decade

and then withdrew when I went through an agitated period, to a few enigmatic cards and a letter from David Foster Wallace; and every flier or poster from many (not all) events where I was invited to read. At home during July days in the upper 90s with similar numbers for humidity, I stood on a concrete floor in a cooler, moderately drier basement, sorting media materials by book, sheathing fragile newspaper clippings in plastic sleeves, and occasionally stopping to read about an author who was "a subversive, anarchistic writer… hardly forgettable," who wrote fictions "remarkable for the force and freedom of

For this page, I had scanned an image of a handwritten letter I received from David Foster Wallace in 1995. At that time, Wallace was a professor at Illinois State University. I had been a finalist for that job, but they made the obvious choice. Wallace's letter followed a reading I'd given at ISU, before which there had been some repartee between us. The letter referenced the banter, with an apology, in case I'd been offended at any comments that were sexualized or gendered (using neither of those words). He also proposed that a mainstream magazine where he was published would be a good venue for my work, and that my reading — or the novel I'd read from — had prompted his friend (identified by name in a context that indicated she was a girlfriend) to suggest he buy a camera. Copyright law says I do not own the prose contents of the letter, but I do own the actual artifact: Mine to sell or frame or include in my archives. Mine as a reminder that he did recommend me to an editor at Harper's, but I was not published there. Mine to represent what I was supposed to accomplish. EXCEPT not in this space. The David Foster Wallace Literary Trust denied me permission to include the image of the letter or to publish it in any form. As though it never happened.

their imaginative style" and from whom "talent jumps off like an overcharge of electricity," but who had—as publicity became author-generated, reviews went digital and review venues extinct—grown more and more invisible, and, apparently, forgettable.

For four years, as 2020 now approaches, the lives of my ancestors and my parents; the memories of my dog and my own childhood; and the (d)evolution of my writing career have all paraded before my perception (aka *passed before my eyes*). Not just watched aghast, but re-lived, re- invented, or psychologically analyzed with questions and guesses: Is it significant that my dad preferred Patton over Eisenhower, and before he died was enthralled with the current source of my need-for-distraction, #45? What did my mom mean when she wrote to my father, early in their marriage, "we probably won't have as many girls"? And could she hear the subtext when she wrote, "I don't care for Jr. but if you like it I do too." Does this explain how she moved from *Leaves of Grass* to Danielle Steele? What were dad's real tacit feelings when his third child was yet another girl, despite my mom's assurance? What was my role in my dog's suffering, and did his crisis impact my ability to feel? How wrought *was* I when the N.Y. editor who had once advocated for me asked my agent if I was dangerous and decided to cut off contact?

Archiving, and the resultant engrossing time-warp, did build and (barely) maintain a sandbag breakwater to keep 2016-2020 from flooding in. It also provided a means to gape at—albeit my own re-creations—the world my grandparents chose to enter, adopt, to sign allegiance to, raise a family in; the one my parents met head-on, embraced, settled into, accepted without question was right (in several meanings of the word); the world I was handed after a Baby-boom childhood—although not given the optimal gender as my mom tried to assure—where debt-free higher education could be had in exchange for putting on a band uniform and blowing through a trombone; and the literary world I was initially welcomed into, where apparently I thrived in a sub-category, until—like my ancestors and their life endeavors that could only be fantasized; and my parents' lifetime of exploits, landscaping projects, paintings and preservation of it all in photographs; and now my own boxed career prolonging the list—time, talent, and tenacity ran their course.

Here's my essay about "how this feels." It feels like dying.

Ask The Depot Commander

He didn't land on a French beach, he didn't crawl through a Pacific jungle, he didn't fly through rising battlefield smoke, he didn't parachute into hostile disputed territory, he didn't stagger out of an enemy POW camp. It seems we always knew that much, just as we knew he had come home with binoculars bearing a swastika, a bronze and stainless-steel chess set machined by German POWs, and green footlockers stamped U.S. Army that went to the Sierras with us every year, packed with campfire cooking equipment. As young adults, we knew he was part of the generation that had faced, stared down, and unified to overcome a one-two punch of desperate financial ruin and a fascist crusade to engulf civilization. He returned from Germany to resume civilian life halfway through 1946 and did exactly what retrospective summaries depict about the deluge of veterans: went back to school, produced a handful of baby boomers, sent them all to almost-free public universities, and prospered in a newly burgeoning middle class that had barely existed in his Brooklyn boyhood.

He didn't tell military stories until we asked. We didn't ask for such a long time. Fifty, fifty-five, sixty years of not asking. The profoundest story now may be in what he still remembers.

He left the University of California in his sophomore year to enlist in the Army after Pearl Harbor. It might be a cliché or an obscene generalization to assume those who were drafted were more quickly sent to infantry, while those who enlisted were trained in a skill, from clerical to technology, from infrastructure and supply to entertainment and propaganda. Still, it was true for him, and from January 1942 to June 1945, from the rank of private in the Army Air Corps through 2nd lieutenant in the Army Signal Corps, he remained on stateside Army bases.

Why didn't you go to Europe <u>during</u> the War?

"Whenever I asked, I was told teaching and training were important too."

11

So as the European theater heightened, moved toward its obvious climax, he felt merely a cog, like tens of thousands of others in the human infrastructure of a world war. Letters to buddies were returned, stamped "deceased."

Did you feel lucky?

"No. I wanted to go."

Finished with officer training in '43, with expertise in radio and communications technology—from carrier pigeons to electronics—he was finally put into an officer-replacement pool between March and June 1945, then landed in France at the end of July. His assignment: prepare and repackage radio equipment being collected from all over Europe to be redeployed in damp climates of Pacific jungles.

But in the middle of August, an "exigent" verbal order abruptly changed his assignment. He was suddenly transferred to Nuremburg, Germany, by command of General Eisenhower: "Verbal orders of the theater Commander, on 20 Aug 1945, relieving the officers named below, on detached service with the 192nd Signal Repair Co and returning them to Hq TSFET (Sig Sec), are made of record, the exigencies of the service having been such to prevent issuance of orders in advance." Upon receipt of the formal written order, 30 August 1945, he had already passed through Reims, France, in route to Frankfort Germany, and then on to Nuremburg.

As early as 1943—six months before D-Day—planning was launched for post-war Europe. At several junctures Allied plan formulation was unduly influenced by U.S. Treasury Secretary Henry J. Morgenthau Jr. whose punitive proposal for post-surrender Germany involved destroying all industrial capability and turning Germany into a purely agricultural, pastoral territory, as well as embracing retributive consequences of ongoing drastic food shortages. In the winter/spring of 1945, the Yalta Conference took place—three months before Hitler's death—to discuss putting the pieces of Europe back together, as well as the problem of Germany itself. While the Morgenthau plan did not become authorized at Yalta, it did continue to influence the eventual Joint Chiefs of Staff policy (JCS 1067) that directed the U.S. occupation to "...take no steps looking toward the economic rehabilitation of Germany [nor steps] designed to maintain or strengthen the German economy."

Immediately after V-E Day on May 8, 1945, redeployment plans went into effect—to transfer men and equipment to the Pacific Theater.

Concurrently, the Potsdam Conference, July to August 2, 1945, would solidify the entire Allied occupation's management of post-war Germany. Among the many world-shaping negotiations and compromises (or conciliations) involving borders, ethnic groups, and the secret-knowledge of what was about to happen in Japan, the conference determined the future of the German economy, and was *still* being influenced by the Morgenthau plan. Thus, all industry that could potentially ever be used for any military purpose was to be destroyed, plus technology and exports would be controlled, with the hope the country would become primarily domestic and agrarian.

Four days after the conference closed, Hiroshima was obliterated by the first atomic bomb. Three days later, the same for Nagasaki. Five days later Japan capitulated to a surrender already outlined in the Potsdam Conference.

No radio equipment would need preparation for the jungles of the Pacific.

The lieutenant's "exigent" order was an assignment as Depot Commander in Nuremburg, Germany, where trains arrived bringing any of the following (and more), switching one to another as 1945 turned to 1946: military equipment confiscated from the German military, German citizens expelled from former Nazi-occupied countries, coal, food, industrial equipment and machinery from dismantled German factories.

The Depot Commander's main assignment, as concerned the U.S. Army, was the sorting, repair and storage of German electrical equipment being collected and shipped to this central location. The Nuremberg depot was transformed into barracks for enlisted men under his command, which included but was not limited to the signal repair corps. His men, however, were not tasked with unloading the trains that arrived daily—and increased in number as more tracks were repaired—with

Signal Repair Depot

Industry and Labor

Certain U.S. Treasury officials working in the occupation—dubbed "Morgenthau boys"—saw to it that JCS 1067 was adhered too as literally and narrowly as possible (i.e. the production of oil, rubber, merchant ships, and aircraft were prohibited).[1] This was occurring even before another plan in 1946 that dictated German industry be lowered to half of 1938 levels, which would have meant the destruction of 1500 plants [2] (undoubtedly those with links to former military use, as well as those that could conceivably do so in the future). It's possible this target was never achieved because by 1950, equipment had been removed from [only] 706 manufacturing plants.[3]

Still, it was happening, and the deconstruction of German industry didn't stop at scrapping machinery. Technologies that were unique or superior to U.S. know-how—from microscopes and electronics to farm chemicals and food manufacturing systems—were collected, either in patent and drawings or actual equipment, and exported back to the U.S.[4] Other machinery and parts from dismantled military-material factories would conceivably go toward rebuilding other manufacturing facilities that had been damaged in Allied bombing. One report was that only 995 industrial plants existed in the American sector, although fuel to run plants was in short supply, and any factory with over 3,000 employees had to be "broken up."[5] Manufacturing—and the coal required to do it—would be needed not only to rebuild German infrastructure but as exports to offset the vital imports of (initially) food and other raw materials. Besides coal, approved exports included leather, alcohol in many forms, musical instruments, textiles, and electrical equipment.[6]

With the influx of hundreds of thousands of Germans leaving former-Nazi-occupied countries, millions of German POWs, and the remaining millions of displaced persons from other devastated European countries, there were far too many people who needed food and shelter and far too few jobs in an economy struggling to re-start.

cargos needing to be sorted, warehoused and/or shipped elsewhere. His men rounded up crews of German civilians who did this work.

Were they Nazis?

"They were free people. Bankers dressed in banking suits showed up to unload trains."

Why?

"For food. Daily work was paid in chits for food."

Like any command post, the depot also needed clerical workers. Two German women were assigned to the Depot Commander. One was a trained drafting technician. The Depot Commander asked her to create a scale map of the depot facility. He also got soap from his appropriation and gave it to the girls, to encourage them to bathe.

Decades later, the Depot Commander would go down to the local high school and demand his eldest daughter take chemistry, not typing.

In addition, there was far too much debris to be cleared and salvaged (sometimes brick by brick). The American military was not engaging in direct restoration, as under JS 1067, "Occupation forces were not to assist with economic development." Therefore, German citizens between 14 and 65 years of age (male) and 15 and 50 years of age (female) were required to register to work in whatever ways were needed or assigned, including road repairs, cleaning and repairing buildings for allied military use, repairing infrastructure, some skilled trades, and shoulder-to-shoulder human lines of bucket-passing extending hundreds of yards where there was no running water (bathing was prohibited or restricted). "The penalty for disobedience was imprisonment and having their ration cards taken away." [5] There is no evidence incarceration was ever used for slackers. Hunger likely was enough motivation.

The Depot Commander & map of facility created by female German drafting technician.

German woman at work in the Depot Commander's office; unknown if this is the drafting technician.

Between 100 and 150 German POWs were also quartered in and worked at the depot, as were the Polish Guard which supervised the POWs. Both were under the authority of the Depot Commander.

It was the Polish Guard that alerted the Depot Commander about a radio being built in the POW quarters. The Depot Commander went to the POW barracks and told the ranking POW officer that he understood a radio was being prepared. The POW captain conceded, did not even attempt a lie. "You understand, I'll have to take it," the Depot Commander said, and the German captain said, yes, he knew that, and forfeited the radio parts.

Did you speak German?

"He spoke enough English."

The simple parts were likely pilfered from cargo being unloaded from trains. The POWs also noticed metal and machinery among the German equipment arriving by train. Their captain asked the Depot Commander if his men could use it to make a chess set, so they could play in their quarters. The Depot Commander said, yes, if they also made one for him and one for his sergeant.

The scrap metal was precision turned into rounded symmetrical stainless steel and bronze pieces. Used for decades by The Depot Commander's future children, who still wonder where the matching sets belonging to the sergeant and the POWs themselves have gone.

POWs

All German military personnel, anywhere, who were alive after the conquest of Berlin in spring 1945, were prisoners. Estimates for their numbers are as high as eleven million. Each of the four Allied powers handled the vanquished German forces differently. In the American sector, none were, technically, POWs. They were prisoners *after* war. Prisoners *for* fighting a war. They were *disarmed enemy forces.*

DEFs did not have the same Geneva Convention rights as POWs. *Prisoners in this category had their personal property impounded without any receipt being given; they had no spokesman to represent them before the Detaining Power; officers received no pay and other ranks, although compelled to work, got no wages. ... Most important of all, these men had no legal status and were at the entire mercy of the victor.* [7]

There have been numerous hypotheses for why the War Department or Eisenhower decided on the new acronym: from technicality (Nazi Germany was no longer a "state" therefore could not be said to have its forces held as prisoners), to reprisal (reversing Germany's own "Hunger Plan" back onto them), to practicality (there weren't enough resources in Europe to feed the entire former Nazi military the same amount as the U.S. troops[8]). Certainly Roosevelt said some unfortunate things: "Let them have soup kitchens, let their economy sink," and, in response to being asked if Germans should starve, "why not?" [9] These quotes were supposed to have happened on March 20, 1945, a few months after a cabinet member told his daughter that he sometimes didn't understand what people said to him, and that he seemed to quickly forget what he was told.[9] Twenty-two days later Roosevelt was dead from a stroke.

At first the estimated 11 million surrendered German military personnel were put to work rebuilding the countries destroyed in the war, including clearing mines, exhuming mass graves, and creating military cemeteries. Archive photos show columns of men marched under guard, each carrying a shovel and a white cross. Initial impoundments of German DEFs, certainly chaotically inhumane, were emptied by September 1945. They were dispersed to where their labor was most needed, based on their skills or previous occupations.

Hand turned metal chess set. Detail on knights and rooks appears to be hand drawn.

Whenever he remembers the Polish Guard, the Depot Commander recollects that each morning at 5 a.m. the Polish unit would march vigorously through the city of Nuremberg.

Did they force the POWs to march?

"No. Just the Guard."

Why?

"They did it to make their presence known."

The Polish Guard in front of the Depot. Note the casual body language of the American to the left.

First-hand stories from surviving citizens have it that for four years, every day at noon, Nazi soldiers marched down the Champs Elysees, accompanied by a Nazi military band. In the second decade of the 21st century, deniers argue that Hitler was sensitive to causing humiliation and did not allow victory parades. However, it's a filmed fact that on October 5, 1939, Nazi soldiers and a military band presented a victory parade for Hitler through the streets of Warsaw, Poland.

Twenty-five years after the Commander woke daily to the Polish Guard's announcement of presence, his children found camaraderie, commitment and the pleasure of collaboration toward a goal in competitive military marching bands.

One of the Commander's children in military band, 1973

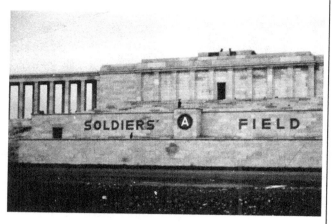

Hitler's Zeppelin Field in 1946 and 1936 (Depot Commander's photo above, Getty images below).

Did you know any Russians?

"They came to the trials to witness them, and some Americans invited them to their clubhouse. The Russians became too familiar with the American officers so they were removed and sent back to Russia and a new contingent was sent. The new Russians didn't associate with Americans."

What caused them to change?

"It was the American occupation zone, and Russia had no business there."

Russia & Justice

On the day President Roosevelt died, or the day after, Eisenhower forbid the armies under his command to continue on toward Berlin. He had actually made the decision weeks earlier, and had even informed Stalin via telegram.[10] Despite disagreement from other generals, notably Patton, Eisenhower would not relent. His reasons were: (1) His armies had already taken all land that would eventually be the American occupation zone, therefore they would take causalities for gaining territory that would be Russia's. (2) Berlin as a goal was political, not military. (3) He had concerns about his troops meeting the Russians "on the run around a corner."[10]

Russian implementation of communist governments in a zone surrounding Russia had been a loophole allowed to exist in the Yalta agreement.[11] As the war was ending, swift Russian mobilization toward this goal was profound. In fact, establishing its footprint in all of its occupied territories, but especially Germany, was fully evident by the time US. Troops arrived in Berlin on July 1.[5] Negotiations and scheming and maneuvering and foisting of new regimes and refusing to acknowledge foisted regimes also began immediately, as did shipping of disassembled German factories from Berlin back to Russia.[5] And in this context of remaking (or reallocating) the world, a "vast symbolic act of collaboration" was to take place: The Nuremberg War-Crimes Trials.[5] It could also be called a *last* symbolic act of collaboration.

Nuremberg was chosen as the location of the trials because it had a large Palace of Justice with an attached prison that had been mostly unscathed in Allied bombing. Of secondary importance was Nuremberg's reputation as the "ceremonial birthplace" of the Nazi Party[12] (or perhaps the birthplace of Nazi ceremony) because it had been the location of annual Nazi propaganda rallies. (And one of those rallies introduced the anti-Semitic Nuremberg Laws.) While Russia had naturally wanted the trials to be in Berlin, a compromise made Berlin the home of the International Military Tribunal authorities.[13] Each of the four allied occupiers contributed one of the four Nuremberg judges.

Did you attend any of the trial?

"Part of my duty was to make sure radio transmissions of the trials made it to the U.S."

Was that amazing to be witnessing history?

"It wasn't history to us at the time. We just wanted to see them punished."

VISITORS' GALLERY
INTERNATIONAL
MILITARY TRIBUNAL

Ralph Mayer

SEAT NO
121
SESSION
224

Nearby the depot was a working factory that manufactured and recycled electronic or telecommunications cable. Unused cable was being gathered and brought there to be made useful again. One day an officious Russian General came to the Depot Commander and asked, "when can we start dismantling the cable works?" The Depot Commander told him, "over my dead body." As long as the Depot Commander was stationed in Nuremberg, through July 1946, the cable factory continued to run.

There were 403 open sessions held in the first round of trials for the worst of the war criminals. The opening statement was 21 November 1945. The verdicts were read on 1 October 1946. The trials were not just concerning the indictments for war crimes or crimes-against-humanity, the defendants were also being accused of "waging aggressive warfare." It was the first time a defeated enemy would be tried for "having committed war" at all.[5]

Summary:
The Signal Corps in the European Theatre
According to the *Occupation Forces In Europe* series, in the second half of 1945, the major duties for the three signal depots in Europe were:

- Repair and packing of Signal equipment for redistribution to the Pacific (curtailed early).
- Redeployment of Signal troops
- Shipments of over 150K tons of signal supplies from western Europe to the U.S. and Germany (mostly concluded by the beginning of April 1946), including disposal of captured Nazi equipment.
- Establishment of permanent signal depots in the U.S. Zone; by the end of June 1946, permanent signal depots had been established at Mannheim, Nuremberg and Munich.

Among ancillary duties, the signal corps established communications for the *Stars and Stripes* and other press services, put in 10 VHF circuits from Altenburg Castle in Bamberg, and furnished the signal communications for the war crimes trails at Nuremberg.

At first the Depot Commander and his four 2nd lieutenants lived at the depot, but they needed to live separately from their men. The Army located a residential area to convert into officers housing. The Depot Commander and his lieutenants would live in a house occupied by two families. The families were told they had to leave.

Did they own the building?

"I don't know. Maybe they rented it."

Where did they go?

"I don't know. But one of their daughters who stayed as a maid asked permission for her parents to come back and get the potatoes they had stored in the basement, so I met them when they did that."

Housing

Early in the occupation, POWs and German citizens had been tasked with refurbishing untouched or only slightly damaged buildings for U.S. military use, including barracks for enlisted men. Finding housing already seemed bleak for German citizens. "The troops and the displaced persons always had first choice," [15] But five or six months into the occupation, the Army began "requisitioning" German housing for officers and American military families. Then it was the displaced persons waiting in line as "... [T]he Special Occupational Planning Board requested major commands to choose sites for communities to be established in their respective areas. ... Among the problems which confronted the Board were disposition of approximately 100,000 displaced persons then residing in forty-five of the chosen military communities." [14]

Depot Commander's officers' quarters

Displaced person (DP) or displaced German citizen

German citizens salvaging furniture in winter 1945-46

20

The two families who vacated the residence when it was appropriated for officers' quarters had, between them, three daughters in their 20s. The three young women were left in the house to serve as domestics for the officers, to earn their food ration. The house had three bedrooms; the Depot Commander had three lieutenants. After the Commander chose a room, he told his lieutenants they could divide the other rooms as they chose. He then told the oldest of the three young women that she would be his domestic, to clean his room and care for his laundry, and the other two women would take care of the other two rooms.

The Depot Commander was a good catholic who would have been taking communion if there had been a way to give a confession. He didn't want to have to store up confessions. So in his room, the Depot Commander placed on his dresser a photo of his cousin, a dark-haired, dark-eyed woman about his age. When his German maid saw the photo she asked, "Is this your girlfriend?"

Fraternization [14]

Prior to VE Day, fraternization with Germans was utterly prohibited, including no conversing (even arguing) which would include all forms of bartering, no visiting German homes, no shaking hands (which seemed to cover all physical contact). A warning in the Army newspaper said, "If you ... bow to a pretty girl or pat a blond child ... you bow to Hitler and his reign of blood."[5]

But nonfraternization policy was, by nature, unattainable. Fraternization meant any social contact, but became code for sexual contact with German women, and VD rates were a means of knowing who violated the rule. After VE Day, these violations flourished. And yet despite the burgeoning need for antibiotics and attempts to continue courts martial for offenders, the Army realized the number of unknown violators by far outstripped its records of known fraternizers. Basically, fraternization continued because no officer had the time, means, or will to attempt a wholesale approach for controlling and punishing offenders. One officer reported that if he had made an issue of every breach by his troops, his entire command would be in jail.

The Occupation Army Chief Historian's report suggested one reason for the difficulty in enforcement of anti-fraternization policy was "the temptations which allegedly were placed before the American soldier by German women. Many persons ... go so far as to say that the moral standards of German girls and women were low or nonexistent." Besides blaming Nazi propaganda for "encouraging illicit sexual relations," the Historian's report does admit that "the abject economic condition of the German population at the time of their defeat is recognized as another factor encouraging" all kinds of fraternization, including, of course, prostitution. "The 'free and easy' attitudes of the German women and her readiness to seek the company of soldiers bearing chocolates and cigarettes in their pockets undoubtedly placed temptation in the way of the American ... It can at least be said that ... German girls were, on the whole, willing to cooperate in his violation of the strict military orders against fraternization."

The Commander took the chance that lying about your cousin would not be a confessable offense in this case. He answered that yes, she was.

"You have a beautiful girl," the German maid said, "we won't take any chances. There won't be any romance."

Why was she assuming there would be a romance?

"She said there *wouldn't* be."

What about the other two maids? Did they have romances?

"Yes, if you could call it romance."

Other forms of fraternization were "comparatively innocent ... such as having laundry and sewing done or other personal services performed." Likewise bartering for German cameras and artwork with Army-rationed cigarettes, gasoline, food and coffee had initiated a military black market, and "almost every contact to obtain a material advantage was, of course, a violation of the rule of nonfraternization." Many new directives were issued in an attempt to stanch the black market exchanges between American soldiers and German citizens. And "when the enforcement of nonfraternization became more of a problem, persons in the field continued to cast about for some method to punish the German partner."

Part of what broke down fraternization rules was the need to employ German citizens. At first German citizens were not going to be used for employment, except when deemed absolutely necessary and then only under strict supervision, and with stringent anti-fraternization policies. The Occupation had assumed displaced persons would want the available employment, but this proved to not develop, so as early as June 1945, hundreds of German civilians were working in the U.S. Army command headquarters. Between July and August 1945, authorization was given for Germans to work in entertainment (bands & orchestras), and—under control of headquarters command—as domestic servants in officers' billets.

Social contact with German children had already been allowed via a statement by General Eisenhower. The remaining nonfraternization rules were eased gradually, many without directives. One way the rule was undermined was an announcement that VD alone would no longer be considered evidence of fraternization. Another form of relaxation was when American soldiers were permitted to "engage in conversation with adult Germans in public." After that no more delinquency reports were made in the Third Army. MPs had orders to make no arrests except in the most flagrant cases (such as rape). As of 1 October 1945, all restrictions on fraternization were lifted except that marriage with Germans and "billeting of American troops with German families" would need authorization from zone commanders.

German children, perhaps orphans, conceivably going to a party.

Christmas [15]

It wasn't until 1946—after the most important judgements handed down in the trials—the U.S. Occupation Army and U.S. citizens in Germany began a tradition of contributing to provide a festive Christmas celebration for German citizens. A year earlier, however, with military guidelines limiting the amount of goodwill Americans or Army personnel were allowed to provide, with tons of debris still lining roads, with food rationed and scarce, Christmas was reduced to kiosks amid the rubble selling cards, red-and-blue pencils, cardboard toys, and "trashy expensive ornaments," parties for German children (since limitations for assistance to children had been eased); and whatever other means of celebration could be foraged.

The Depot Commander with his camera, photo by Herb Schlesinger

In December 1945 the Depot Commander's Sargent—Herb Schlesinger—told him that a local shop, a "manufacturer of Leica cameras," was selling out their stock of the finest German optics. So the commander paid $200 for a new 35mm camera from Stoll Precision Engineering Workshop. (Leica headquarters were in Wetzlar, Germany, some 285 km north).

He used the camera to take photos of the ruins, rubble and signs of German life in the areas in and around Nuremberg.

Is that where you learned darkroom technique?

"No. My sergeant did it. I didn't bother to learn."

Sgt. Schlesinger obtained darkroom equipment and set up a darkroom at the depot. He developed his own plus the Depot Commander's film, made prints, and then printed selected enlargements for the Commander. Sgt. Schlesinger took all his darkroom equipment home with him.

Did you ever see your sergeant again?

"I went to his wedding."

In graduate school in the early 50s, Herb Schlesinger met a girl and was showing her his photos from occupied Germany. She recognized a man in many of his photos as a boy she'd gone to high school with. So the sergeant was able to invite his former commanding officer to his wedding. Four months later the Commander heard the girl had divorced the sergeant. The Commander did not have further contact with his sergeant until 1991 when the commander was invited to the sergeant's extravaganza banquet 70th birthday party.

The Depot Commander had returned to the U.S. and resumed classes at the Univ. of California in 1946. He used his Leica to take photos of the little town of Berkeley, the "card stunt" section in the football stadium, and later to document a trip to Yosemite in 1950. Possibly regretting "not bothering" to learn to develop film, the commander went to a photo equipment company and traded some extra lenses he'd brought home for an enlarger and a movie camera.

On his honeymoon in 1951, the Depot Commander took photos of his new wife, and then, gradually, the Leica became her camera and produced 20-plus years of slides chronicling a family of five babyboomers. The movie camera likewise preserved 1950s Yosemite by horseback, honeymoon scenery of 1951 California out a Studebaker window, babies crawling, pushing toy wheelbarrows, playing with white bunnies, crying on an excursion to play in snow, and birthday parties—the last movie taken in 1963. The enlarger was given, probably unused, to one of the five children when 1970s college journalism introduced silver emulsion photography.

Sergeant Dr. Herbert Schlesinger PhD
This particular sergeant had a college degree from Brooklyn College [where this author would attend a graduate program]. Apparently not all war era college graduates chose to attend officer training. Herb's graduate studies in psychology and psychoanalysis waited until after his Army service in France and Germany. He finished his PhD in 1953, began work in psychoanalysis in Kansas, became head of an adult psychology unit, then moved on to be a professor of psychiatry in Colorado before returning to New York to head a clinical psychology training program and eventually become professor of clinical psychology at Columbia University. He authored at least seven books and numerous joint-authored articles. His biography on the Columbia University website is, as of this writing, still in present tense.

Sgt. Herbert Schlesinger and his new camera. (Sgt Schlesinger may also appear in the photo of the signal depot sign.)

Do you know where you got the Nazi binoculars?

"It's hard to remember 70 years ago. I can't even remember yesterday."

But they were certainly not purchased from any German shop. He never smoked, so he had plenty of cigarettes to trade, usually with other American soldiers who had already acquired booty, perhaps nefariously.

The Nazi binoculars were not likely to be used for sight-seeing. Perhaps the Depot Commander shipped them home (to his parents' address) as soon as they were acquired. He kept all of his receipts for shipped items, but none gives any specifics for what was in the package, only how much he paid for insurance, the most being fifty cents.

The binoculars are actually German Kriegsmarine Leitz U-Boat binoculars. The Depot Commander's children used them from windows of their Southern California hillside home to try to read lighted signs in Tijuana (too little magnification for that), to watch the glow of approaching wildfires, even to monitor the high school marching band's rehearsals in the school parking lot on inopportune sick-days.

The Nazi binoculars and detail on case (below)

Who is in this photo and what is he doing?

"I don't know why he's out of uniform. It's a radio of some kind."

Is this the radio being built by the Germans?

"That radio was being made with razor blades. It couldn't send but only receive, but they weren't allowed any communication, so it was my duty to take radios away."

```
SIGNAL REPAIR CO. 9049                              DECEMBER 18TH, 1945.
NURNBERG GERMANY.


        TO:

                RALPH V. MAZZA
                1ST LT.SIG.C.
                COMMANDING.


        DEAR SIR,

                THE SIGNAL REPAIR CO. 9049 (POW) KINDLY
        ASK YOU TO ACCEPT THEIR INVITATION FOR THEIR
        CELEBRATION OF CHRISMAS EVE ON DECEMBER 24TH 1945
        1900 O'CLOCK IN THE POW-MESSHALL. THE PROGRAM OF THE
        CELEBRATION IS ENCLOSED.
```

                                S. Karell

                        HAUPTMANN AND CO.LEADER

*Invitations to the Depot Commander from the German
DEA captain, referring to his group as POWs.*

```
SIGNAL REPAIR COMP 9049              NUERNBERG,25.DEZEMBER 45




        DEAR SIR,

        ON ACCOUNT OF THE OPENING OF THE READING ROOM
FOR THE PRISONERS OF WAR WE INTEND TO ARRANGE TODAY
1900 O,CLOCK A LITTLE CELEBRATION WITH READING OF LITERATURE
AND POETRY OF OUR OWN WORKS.

        IT WOULD BE A GREAT PLEASURE FOR US IF YOU WOULD
JOIN THIS LITERARY READING EVENING AND ACCEPT OUR INVITATION
FOR IT
```

                                S. Karell

                HAUPTMANN AND KOMP.LEADER

Hauptmann Karrell

Viktor Karell [16] was born in 1898 in the town of Doupov in Bohemia, which became part of the Czech Republic after the war. Before the war, Doupov was a German town with a nearly 100% German population (1600 out of 1620). Immediately following the German surrender, approximately 40 adult males were tortured and killed, presumably by the 20 citizens who were not German, or perhaps by a Russian occupying army. After expelling all Germans in the early 50s, the whole town was replaced by a military training site which now has a population of zero, as it is defunct. The German Wikipedia website lists among the defunct town's "parents," a Viktor Karell, writer and "Germanist."

Viktor served in the Austro-Hungarian army in World War I, then returned to his studies. In 1930, Viktor, a scholar and professor, still lived in Bohemia, teaching and working as an archivist for his doomed home town. He was recruited again for war in 1942 when he was 44 years old. He might have been stationed in Italy. He became a prisoner there and also reached the rank of captain (*Hauptmann*). In any of his German bios on German websites, even clumsy computer translation tools don't hide that his time as a POW is given in one sentence, not even giving the name of the city in which he was held.

After being released in 1946, he achieved his modicum of German fame for founding the first Bavarian junior high school, which is now named for him. His numerous publications, mostly about his hometown and Bavarian areas of Germany (where Nuremberg is central), include *The Poets of the Bohemian Forest*, but do not include any books of poetry or books about either war.

In 1946, The Depot Commander was promoted to the rank of Captain. On a three page rationale, dated in January, the division's Major included a bigger picture. Although the Commander was "... the best fitted officer available for the grade and position for which promotion is recommended," it also seemed prudent for the major to mention that "All officers under my jurisdiction, serving in grades higher than is warranted by the duties and responsibilities of their positions, have been reassigned or have been reported as surplus to the needs of this assignment." Translation: *I need another captain, even though he'll continue to do the work he did as a lieutenant.*

The officers in the depot had a larger alcohol ration than the enlisted men, so the Depot Commander asked his officers, "would you like to share with the men?" He suggested they create a club at the depot where the men could have their beer more inexpensively than in town. The officers agreed and pooled their alcohol rations, which procured delivery of barrels of beer to the club they created in a room at the depot. It was the third special room the Commander carved out of the depot facilities.

One day in his office, the Depot Commander heard a shot, followed immediately by screaming. He bolted from his chair and found, right outside his door, an enlisted man, a replacement into the occupying forces, with blood pouring from a gunshot in his neck. The Depot Commander tried to stop the bleeding, but the wound was severe and the soldier lost consciousness then died there in the hall in the Commander's arms before any medic could be called.

Men (and women, but mostly men) [15]

In the few months between the German and Japanese surrenders, plans were also being hastily completed for redeployment of troops. A point-system, earned via service-months, overseas-months, and battle participation, would determine who went where: home, to the Pacific, or remain in Germany. The highest points got the trip home, but after V-J day there weren't enough transport ships in enough harbors to get the numbers home who had been promised, and now redeployment to the Pacific was curtailed as well. "[E]veryone wanted to go home faster than any feasible schedule could move them and with an intensity that was not going to lie diverted by any amount of persuasion." Hundreds of thousands of American troops were in a hurry-up-and-wait limbo. Before V-J day, educational programs had been developed at colleges throughout Europe, and while only a few tens of thousands took advantage of the classes, after V-J day many colleges closed the program for lack of participation (participants also manipulated course failure so they could be sent back to their units, now waiting to be shipped home).

And yet troop departure from Germany continued to be sluggish, followed by an epidemic of low morale and bad behavior (often the latter classified as the former). Attacks, robberies, rapes and "accidents" perpetrated by U.S. military personnel became a point of concern. "The Office of Military Government for Bavaria described the death of a German boy in a hunting accident involving soldiers as 'a result of such carelessness as to be almost criminal.'"

"By mid-summer 1945, the search for morale-sustaining devices was being stretched to, and perhaps somewhat beyond, the limits of feasibility."

The problem extended into the actual occupation forces—those not waiting to go home but now deployed there to do the job of occupying. An assessment in November 1945 reported the occupying Army was overly proportioned with men "poorly trained in their duties."

Photo of a gun found when never-printed negatives were discovered in film cans in the Commander's basement workbench. Best ID possible from this photo is a German Sauer. It appears to be lying on bedding of some sort.

Since the same report said "A trained, balanced force of infantry armor and air and supporting combat troops no longer exists," and the majority of occupation forces were not armed at all, it was fortunate the surrender had been so absolute that U.S. casualties likely were close to zero during the occupation; any of the scant data on occupation casualties gives credit to the almost complete lack of insurgent resistance in the American sector.

If enough entertainment and diversion could not be supplied, at least the Army could provide the occupying forces "necessities" like cigarettes and beer. "The enormous numbers involved ... made it impossible to do more than supply basic rations, such as tobacco, candy, toilet articles, and beer and Coca-Cola." In fact, "the Army exchange itself supervised production of beer, soft drinks, and ice cream, using German facilities as much as possible."[14]

It was a self-inflicted wound and the culprit was a German pistol, a souvenir the 18-year-old boy had recently traded for. He was a member of the signal repair corps, so his immediate commanding officer, one of the Depot Commander's lieutenants, had to write the letter to the boy's parents.

But the Depot Commander made an order: "Get an [ordinance] artificer over here." An artificer disassembles, repairs, and reassembles ordnance of all types. "Make every German gun in the depot inoperable," the Depot Commander said to his junior officer, "so you won't have to write any more letters."

Was that the last war casualty in the American sector in Europe?

"It was the only one I knew of."

Twenty-five years later, dove-hunting with shotguns, the Commander's excited 12 year old son pivoted to follow flying game and peppered his older sister's jaw with a few stray buckshot. In future family mirth over the incident, including a perplexed dentist who saw shot still embedded in the daughter's gums on an Xray, his children never knew what the commander's first thoughts may have been when the hunting accident happened. We never asked. But the Depot Commander likely did not flashback to the dying soldier in his arms.

The Depot Commander saved his concert bills, and gave ratings (up to five stars) for each piece of music. No concert bill before March 24, 1946 remains; perhaps it took until then to reassemble musicians. The *Nurenburg* [sic] *Philharmonic Orchestra* felt free enough to schedule an all-Beethoven program in April 1946. The Pastoral earned four stars. Five stars had been garnered (on other bills) only by Haydn and Rimsky-Korsakov.

Music

Four days after the official surrender, the U.S. Military Government formed an Information Control Division (ICD), and precisely one month after the surrender a document was released requiring anyone involved with printing, broadcast, theater or music to register with authorities. When it came to classical music, the ICD said, "It is above all essential that we should not give the impression of trying to regiment culture in the Nazi manner. Such an attempt would in any case be doomed to failure. German musical life must be influenced by positive rather than negative means, i.e. by encouraging what we think beneficial and crowding out what we think dangerous."[17] Still, the ICD screened and approved every concert program. Beethoven was one of the only composers particularly named in the document, as his music had been featured in Nazi assemblies and Nazi radio had broadcast part of *Eroica* when announcing Hitler's suicide.[18] The ICD's plan to "crowd out" undesirable music, rather than outright prohibiting it, strongly recommended composers censored by the Nazis, particularly Hindemith, Offenbach and Mendelssohn, whose work was featured when the Berlin Philharmonic gave its first concert in the occupation on May 26. The Nuremburg Symphony Orchestra's website says it was founded in 1946, although the organization's history says nothing about there being an occupation at the time.

NURNBERG ★ OPERA HOUSE
Lt. Leigh B. Bardsley   T/5 Bill Wolfram
SPECIAL SERVICE OFFICER   NON-COM IN CHARGE

Sunday, April 14 – 1400 Hours
SYMPHONY CONCERT
Nurnberg Philharmonic Orchestra
Conductor: *Rolf Agop*
Soloist: *Stefan Proegel*

Ludwig van Beethoven:
4★ *Overture to the Ballett*
      "The Creatures of Prometheus"
      Opus 43, (composed 1801)
            Adagio – Allegro molto con brio
5★ *Romance F Major for Violin and Orchestra*
      Opus 50, (composed 1802)
            Adagio cantabile
4★ *6th Symphony F Major "Pastoral-Symphony"*
      Opus 68, (composed 1808)
            Allegro ma non troppo
            ("Cheerful impressions arriving the country")
            Andante molto moto
            ("Scene on a small river")
            Allegro
            ("Happy time for the peasant")
            Allegro
            ("Thunderstorm")
            Allegretto
            ("Song of the shepherl; happy and than
                        feelings after the storm")

Coming Sunday, April 21 - 14.00 hours
      Great Symphony Concert with 200 people choir;
Anton Bruckner: 6th Symphony A Major
                  150th Psalm
      Nurnberg Philharmonic Orchestra / Conductor: Rolf Agop
                  Soloist: Maria Scarbath

1st. BN 26th Inf. Regt. Special Service

German acrobats entertaining troops did not get a starred rating system.

29

In the Army, the Depot Commander had already learned to hate scrambled eggs, oatmeal, and white gravy poured over anything. The rest of his life he never once ordered the American staple biscuits-and-gravy, too reminiscent of SOS.

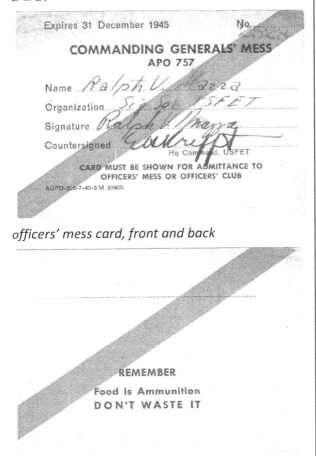

officers' mess card, front and back

The Depot Commander had a fishing license dated 10 December 1945, issued by the Office of Military Government. In addition to bag limits, the license stipulated: "Hunters will not endanger the lives of civilians or troops at any time by careless shooting." And: "Hunters will not enter into conversational conversation with civilians on farms or in forests."

Sustenance

The world did not have enough food. For seven years, tens of millions of men had not been working in any food industry. Hundreds of thousands of European crop acres had been devastated or left fallow. Untold numbers of livestock, farm machinery, and market logistics had been obliterated. Tens of thousands of German butcher shops, bakeries, groceries, market stalls and booths, if they still existed, had barely anything to sell. All over Europe, but especially in Germany, there was little employment to obtain money to buy what little was offered or could be found on the black market. The world was still rationing. Now German citizens and POWs had their shares determined by the victors.

Army occupation orders included: *You will estimate requirements of supplies necessary to prevent starvation or widespread disease ... Such estimates will be based upon a program whereby the Germans are made responsible for providing for themselves, out of their own work and resources. You will take all practicable economic and police measures to assure that German resources are fully utilized and consumption held to the minimum in order that imports may be strictly limited and that surpluses may be made available for the occupying forces and displaced persons ..., and for reparation. You will ... take appropriate measures to ensure that basic living standards of the German people are not higher than those existing in any one of the neighboring United Nations ...*[5]

Estimates for the number of daily calories rationed to non-POW Germans in the second half of 1945 range between 700 and 1250. It is unclear if there even would have been surplus from strictly German-produced food that could then supply the 2300[19] calories allocated to displaced persons (of which estimates go as high as 40 million). The actual calorie ration-formula for German citizens fluctuated during the first two years of occupation, and also was seldom adhered to: from 2150, the estimated average during the prewar depression, to 1500 in the first directive for the occupation.[19]

Eisenhower's deputy, Lt. General Clay explained, "... the Germans should suffer from →

30

It was during a conversational conversation with the foreman at the cable factory that the Depot Commander was invited to go fishing.

The Foreman of the cable factory, fishing, assisted by his wife.

The fishing trip either preceded or followed the two oranges the Depot Commander gave to the foreman for his wife and child.

Where did you get the oranges?

"I asked the mess hall officer for them."

Some-time later, perhaps while on the fishing trip, the foreman told the Depot Commander that his wife and child had eaten one orange section every day. The two oranges lasted more than a week.

In the early 1960s, when the fruit trees in the Commander's yard were still sticks, seven peaches were brought home from the store each week. Each of the Commander's family members got one peach, and when it was gone, had to wait until the following week for the next batch of seven. When his tangerine tree was young and just starting to fruit, the Commander's children got one, then later two tangerines in their Christmas stockings.

hunger and from cold as I believe such suffering is necessary to make them realize the consequences of a war which they caused ... [However] this type of suffering should not extend to the point where it results in mass starvation ..."[19]

By November 1945, perhaps Clay felt the punitive suffering he'd proscribed had been accomplished, as he attempted to alleviate the situation by announcing an allocation of 1500 calories in the American sector. Typically, this was 5-1/2 slices bread, 3 medium potatoes, 3 Tbl oatmeal, 1 tsp fat, 1 tsp sugar. [15]

He accomplished this with imports of food from the U.S., with distribution still regulated. By March of 1946, with imported supplies exhausted, Clay had to reduce daily calories to 1180, and to meet that level had to release corn products in German rations. Corn and corn flour had not previously been part of rations supplied to Germans; they did not consider it fit for human consumption, and viewed its appearance in their provisions a new act of retribution. [15]

Despite U.S. Army-sponsored Christmas parties for children and soup kitchens using Army equipment[15] (and presumably Army food), U.S. military personnel were encouraged, or ordered, not to give food to German citizens. *Notice to U.S. Troops. American taxes pay for your food—it is forbidden to give, sell, or trade it to natives.*[20] This was a poster in mess halls. Sagas are plentiful of spoiled or stale food being rendered inedible via gasoline, burning, or dumping into sewers, and a more specific legend: pouring cocoa into gutter drains in front of hungry German children. [20]

And yet more documented are the packages sent home by U.S. military: "... cameras, Zeiss binoculars, Meissen china, silver, jewelry—whatever was not too hot or [was] too heavy for luggage. In return Germans, or some of them, got food and coffee," [5] or money to buy them on the black market.

The Depot Commander's promotion may not have been official until after February 1946, and he may have missed the Christmas day sharing of literature in the POW's new reading room. On 19 February 1946, Hauptmann Viktor Karell used the same "mill" (all-caps) typewriter—typically used by radio operators—to copy a poem. He then put it into an envelope and addressed it to the Depot Commander, still a 1st Lieutenant. (The rest of Viktor's handwritten one-sentence message, dated on the 21st birthday of the Commander's future wife, remains a mystery.)

Viktor's poem, a song of longing for all of the beautiful places in Italy he had presumably seen while stationed there, was given to an Italian-American Army Captain who wouldn't see those places for over 40 years, when he retired from his college teaching profession and toured Italy with his wife. The Depot Commander could get along with simple German phrases, spoken in necessity, but couldn't read literary German. Looking at the first stanza now, even crudely translated by a robot, someone a generation removed can imagine that Viktor might not have realized the tacit universal mood he was exposing.

```
     _BILDER_AUS_DEM_SUEDEN._            From 1st Lt R. Mezza
        VON DR. VIKTOR KARELL
              1.                               J Karell
                                                19.12.46.
      _BELLAGIO_AM_COMERSEE___
 HIER SCHWEIGT DAS LEID -EIN PARADIES STEHT OFFEN
 UND WINKT DICH IN DER SELIGEN GEFILDE.
 DAS MUEDE HERZ,ES WILL AUFS NEUE HOFFEN
 UND GLAUBT ANS GLUECK VOR DIESEM EDLEN BILDE.
```

It is perhaps a credit to Viktor's character—his love of beauty as well as for his homeland of Bohemia, his belief in and work for education—that he never wrote about life as a POW in the American sector of occupied Germany; and, as far as research can tell, never again wrote about Italy. It looks like he put his war papers, photos and memories aside upon his release in 1946, as did the Depot Commander.

> Here is the silent sorrow—a paradise is open
> And beckons in the blessed realm.
> The tired heart, it wants to hope again
> And believe in happiness before this noble picture.

Do you remember the captain of the prisoners?
> "He was a nice man."

Sources

[1] Petrov, Vladimir. *Money and Conquest; Allied Occupation Currencies in World War II* (1967)

[2] Wallich, Henry C. *Mainsprings of the German Revival* (1955)

[3] Gareau, Frederick H. "Morgenthau's Plan for Industrial Disarmament in Germany." (1961)

[4] Smith, Jean Edward. "American Exploitation of Postwar Germany." (1993)

[5] Davidson, Eugene. *The Death and Life of Germany: An Account of the American Occupation* (1959)

[6] Martin, James Stewart. *All Honorable Men* (1950).

[7] Convention (III) relative to the Treatment of Prisoners of War. Geneva, 12 August 1949.

[8] Ambrose, Stephen E. *New York Times* Feb 24, 1991

[9] Taylor, Frederick. *Exorcising Hitler: The Occupation and Denazification of Germany*

[10] Harsch, Joseph. *Christian Science Monitor*, (April 10, 1995)

[11] *The Yalta Conference.* The Latin Library

[12] Overy, Richard. *Interrogations: The Nazi Elite in Allied Hands*, (2001).

[13] "Rough Notes Meeting with Russians." Kew, London: Lord Chancellor's Office, Public Record Office. 29 June 1945

[14] "First Year of Occupation" and "Fraternization with the Germans in World War II." U.S. Army Historical Division, European Command. (1947)

[15] Ziemke, Earl F. *The U.S. Army In The Occupation of Germany 1944-1946.*

[16] all from a sparsely completed German Wikipedia sites, translated by Google, citations all in German or Czech.

[17] "Draft Guidance on the Control of Music," 8 June 1945

[18] Anderson, Abby E. *Music Among the Ruins: Classical Music, Propaganda and the American Cultural Agenda 1945-49.*

[19] Wiggers, Richard Dominic. "The U.S. and the Refusal to Feed German Civilians after WWII." (2003)

[20] Cherny, Andrei. *The Candy Bombers: The Untold Story of the Berlin Airlift and America's Finest Hour*

Supported throughout via images by the film: *After Hitler*, David Korn-Brzoza and Olivier Wievioka. And *Occupation Forces in Europe* (www.usarmygermany.com).

Photos of the Depot Commander were probably taken by his sergeant, Herb Schlesinger. Other photos of 1945-46 Nuremberg are by Ralph Mazza, Captain, U.S. Army Signal Corps, 1945-46, unless otherwise notated as stock photos.

Camera: A Life-Partner

Having Pictures

A moment that was happy, funny, accomplished, interesting, dramatic, successful, meaningful, beautiful, blissful, sublime: Mom wanted a photo—she needed to *take* a photo—to ensure she would be able to *keep* those and other unnamable feelings.

I've known people whose parents didn't leave them with stacks of albums and drawers of slides. One, the son of a professional portrait photographer whose "family shots" fit (and were stored) in one shoebox. And another whose parents were raised on dry-farms, so the concept of buying a camera and paying for processing and printing was in the same privileged realm as having a housekeeper. I've

> Admittedly, it was easier to look at this phenomenon before every phone had a camera (usually filled with hundreds, if not thousands of photo files, most never looked at again).

also known of people whose parents may in fact have left them a middle-class cache of snapshots and slides, but who themselves didn't seek to document every (even trivial) milestone or new vista (even in their own backyard) with a photo.

It *may* affect those of us with always-camera-equipped parents more. It also may affect our reminiscences of childhood—the collective one and the differing individual memories. Is my memory of childhood *better* than that son-of-a-photographer, or just different? Is my drift into nostalgia more gauzy? Mine doesn't even compare to the fanciful memories of the friend whose parents didn't own a camera until he was 8 or 9. Yet maybe not only the existence

> "People have to think about arranging the picture and they have to focus the camera. This effortful processing should improve memory. But that isn't what [researchers have] found..." Taking pictures seems to put our cognitive effort into the photograph and not our personal memory. Reviewing pictures may help memory, but may also replace memory."
> Ira Hyman Ph.D. *Psychology Today*, December 30, 2013

> "A photo-taking-impairment effect has been observed such that participants are less likely to remember objects they photograph than objects they only observe."
> Julia S. Soares, Benjamin C. Storm, "Forget in a Flash," *Journal of Applied Research in Memory and Cognition*, 2017

of Mom's photos, but the reverent care and viewing of photos *have* added dimensions to my memoires. I can be wistful not just about hot chocolate in tin cups around a campfire in the Sierras, but also about evenings in the living room with photos of Sierra

camping projected onto a sparkle-textured screen—five kids and parents engaged in something we called "having pictures." One of us might ask, "Mom, can we have pictures tonight?" Or if Mom had just gotten a new box of slides back from the processor, one of us would shout down the hall to those diligently doing homework, "We're having pictures!"

> "In families, reviewing pictures can serve as a scaffold that enables conversations about the past with children. In this way, pictures can strengthen both memory and relationships."
> Ira Hyman Ph.D. *Psychology Today*, December 30, 2013

Viewing the slides as a family may work the same way as taking photos: there are photographed events from my 1st decade I don't remember, except to remember the slide; and a few *un*photographed events that I *do* recall with clear brain-images: We were going to have a "cookout," a barbecue on the patio of the tract house in a mass-produced neighborhood. Already outside at the picnic table, I saw Mom come through the sliding door with a tray holding everything we would need: hotdogs, condiments, even the special salt-and-pepper shakers only used at barbecues because they were pigs with chef hats who oinked when turned upside-down and shaken. Then Mom's feet went wrong or tangled in something, and she went down. I

think remember Mom crying. I *do* remember the spattered trail of mustard and ketchup on the patio, as though I have it on Kodachrome. I also remember we did not have that barbecue. But for another cookout, despite being in our new and "forever" house not in a subdivision, where cookouts were like camp, I only remember the photograph and that it was something we did more than once, but I don't specifically remember the actual event(s).

With my own photo-enhanced and photo-impaired memory examples, I am only speculating about Mom's, and about her relationship not only with her cameras but with the tangible images she could keep.

> "[P]sychology research has shown that under some conditions taking a photo of something actually makes it harder to remember. … [R]esearch on transactive memory … shows that longtime partners or friends distribute memory demands between them, creating a 'shared' system where one will remember certain things so the other doesn't need to. … [I]n a similar fashion we may be treating the camera as a memory partner and offloading the effort onto it."
>
> Alex Fradera, The British Psychological Society, May 31, 2018,

First Friends: Jiffy & Brownie

With her camera's help, Mom kept captioned albums (at the time called *scrap books*—two words) from 14-years-old through 25, when she switched mostly to color slides. The earliest album has black-and-white (now brown and tan) rectangular photos—perhaps taken by a Kodak *Jiffy*—glued directly to black paper pages which would someday crack, break and crumble. Later albums' square photos, from a Kodak Brownie (see photo above and here) joined the rectangular shots. Both were stuck onto the same kind of black pages with lick-to-stick photo corners. She never seemed to mind handing her camera to someone else so she could have

photos of herself participating in occasions, which might make the camera even more of a "partner." In fact, there's evidence of a first-generation (1944) selfie, based on the hint of angle of Mom's arms, the look of trepidation on her friend's face, and how close the camera is—it's doubtful a person would stand that close and there was no zoom lens capability on the era's simpler cameras.

The dimensions of this selfie suggest it was taken with the Kodak Jiffy, not the easier-to-use Brownie. But there could be a missing camera from Mom's college years.

In summer of 1946, Mom and her parents plus an aunt and uncle headed west from Boston in a car. Mom was starting her first teaching job in California in the fall; and Mom's brother, a minister in California whose connections had gotten her that job, was getting married. The trip was preserved in a photo album, not always in geographical order—the first four pages of Niagara Falls are *followed* by the Finger Lakes—with 6x9 cm photos from the Kodak Jiffy. The trip continued into Ohio, dropped south to follow the Lincoln Highway and old U.S. 40 through Illinois, Iowa, and Nebraska—with a few amazed photo captions like "farm," "cattle," "corn," and "road is straight for miles." Then into Colorado where Mom enjoyed (i.e. photographed) the Rocky Mountains followed by Utah's National Parks, Bryce and Zion, the Grand Canyon, and on into San Diego where Mom didn't yet know she would photograph her five children growing up. Most of her photos from that trip are landscapes, and most, therefore, fairly poor. Probably without realizing how her shots would turn out, she began augmenting her preservation of the trip with original B&W photographs—not postcards—sold in gift shops, starting in Niagara Falls where the souvenir photos were about an inch-and-a-half by one-inch, then the stunning (by a someday-well-known photographer?) shots in the National Parks.

Mom's landscapes above, Rocky Mountains and Grand Canyon. Professional souvenir photos below.

"View from El Tovar" - Grand Canyon Nat'l. Park

The rectangular format photos of the Jiffy mostly give way to the square of the Brownie after the album shifts from the trip west to Mom's documentation of her fall 1946 activities as a physical education teacher at a private boarding school. And yet it's the Brownie around her neck before that in a college photo, and the formats remain mixed—with a preference for the Brownie—through 1951. Photos from both cameras, taken by Mom, also show up in her mother's photo albums where Nana saved all the photos sent by her children. Mom might see her mother every 2 or 3 years; long distance telephone was expensive. Probably every letter

In an interview Dr Rachel Hershenberg, licensed clinical psychologist, explained two types of shared experience: 1. Sharing an experience in reality with another person. "It can maximize how much you enjoy the event while strengthening the bond you feel for one another because →

Mom wrote to her mother and sister was accompanied by photos to illustrate her description of places, events, and children growing up. To have *seen* the same thing is part of a closer bond.

In 1971, before we embarked on a 6-week trip across the country in a camper, Mom gave the Jiffy to one of my sisters. To me she gave her father's InstaFlex, the kind where you hold the camera at your waist and look down into a series of mirrors. To my brother, a box camera, possibly a Brownie. And to my eldest sister, a brand new Instamatic.

> you participated in it together." And 2, having an experience then telling someone else about it.
> https://bit.ly/3cGBdvl
> But what if the telling is augmented by sharing a photograph of part of the event? Wouldn't that almost be a blend of 1 & 2? Wouldn't the person hearing about an event and seeing a photo be sharing more than a subjective description but have the opportunity to have a fragment of an individual perception, and thus have a stronger "sharing"?

When Partners Fail

On that 1971 Interstate expedition, even though each of us had our own camera, Mom and Dad took slides that became the family record. But apparently there was some malfunction or film-loading disaster. From a week spent in North Carolina there are 42 slides, followed by 55 slides of Williamsburg and Washington DC. But then in Boston/Cape Cod—where we visited Mom's parents' and family, and the places she grew up—there are all of 10 slides. Even worse, one of the pinnacles of the trip was Southport Maine where Mom's grandfather and great-grandfather had been the lightkeepers at Hendrick's Head. Over several days we rowed dories, did graveyard rubbings, treasure-hunted at extreme low tides, and visited the lighthouse. There are *seven* slides from Maine. What could have happened? The most likely answer: Sometimes 35mm film didn't engage in the camera's sprockets when loaded, so it wouldn't advance when wound after each shot. Mom could spend a week taking pictures, wondering why she wasn't getting to the end of the roll, only to discover the roll had never started.

Not a coincidence, then, that only months after that trip, for Christmas 1971, Dad bought Mom a new Minolta rangefinder—she could still choose aperture and speed, still had to focus, but it did not allow for changing lenses. For 10 more years she still mostly took slides, but for the first time she could take slides indoors.

Autofocus compact cameras were introduced in 1977. These had mechanized zoom lenses, auto exposure and focus. Mom returned to print film and left slides completely in 1982. She had a series of cameras that could provide clear (or clear enough) action-stopping

Dad is making sure Mom uses her new camera correctly; indoor photography arrives.

freeze frames of about 20 years of retirement—holidays, family events, gardens, and mostly trips and cruises—leading to approximately 40+ magnetic self-stick photo albums. Some of those cameras were broken, some used their batteries too quickly, one was stolen out of the camper, one sank in the Mediterranean.

In 1993, Mom and Dad went on a cruise in the Mediterranean. Not a banquet-eating, ballroom-dancing cruise; it was an Elderhostel trip. Now known as Road Scholars, these are educational tours planned around topics from nature to earth sciences to history to art or literature, including some classroom lectures, plus hands-on activities and on-site expeditions. On this excursion, the topic was ancient Greek myth and literature. A cruise among the Greek Islands was part of the course. Passengers included twenty Americans and nine crew members on a 32-meter wooden vessel named *"Zeus V."*

One morning, a lecture on the Greek deities was interrupted by an odor of smoke and an instruction to go immediately to the sun deck. There crew members issued life jackets and assisted the Americans in putting them on. The engines were dead. The absence of the constant churn produced a new sort of stillness that magnified the slap of water against the hull, clarified the crisp Greek dialogue exchanged between the busy crew, then called attention to the drone of a car ferry, the *Apollo Express*, approaching the bow.

The car ferry, which had been on its usual route between islands when it spotted the smoke, had veered from its course and was already drawn up alongside the *Zeus V*. With a Greek crew member on each side, the Americans, outfitted in bulky lifejackets, were assisted in making the leap from their cruise vessel to the ferry's deck.

Most of the crew stayed behind on the *Zeus V*, attempting to save the vessel, but the *Zeus V* continued to smolder. Twinkles of flame flickered in the smoke, the flames grew, remained visible longer, finally stood upright and lashed in the wind. Fishing vessels now drew up alongside the burning boat to take on the remainder of the *Zeus V* crew. Shortly afterwards the cruise vessel burned itself out as it sank into the Mediterranean.

Without any of their personal possessions, the Americans were carried to a mainland port on the car ferry, a trip that took until 8 p.m. Unanimously they voted to continue their tour of Greek antiquity on the mainland, and they did so, after a day spent shopping to replace clothes and toiletries, faxing doctors in the States to replace medications and corrective lenses, and (for my mother) searching for postcards or gift books that carried the sights and scenes that were still on the film in her camera that now lay somewhere under the Mediterranean. As she had watched the cruise vessel burn and sink, she probably exclaimed, "Oh, honey, I forgot my camera."

Instead of photos of the fire, she kept the Greek newspaper articles.

Originally appeared in longer form in *Indigenous: Growing Up Californian*
by Cris Mazza (City Lights Books, 2003).

Τουρίστες σώθηκαν μέσα από τις φλόγες

Μικρό κρουαζιερόπλοιο βυθίστηκε μεταξύ Σίκινου και Ιου, όταν εξερράγη πυρκαγιά στο μηχανοστάσιο

«Τέλος καλό όλα καλά», για τους επιβάτες και το πλήρωμα του ελληνικού τουριστικού σκάφους «ΖΕΥΣ 5» που τυλίχθηκε στις φλόγες, χθες το πρωί, στη θαλάσσια περιοχή μεταξύ Σίκινου και Ιου. Προς βοήθειαν έσπευσε αμέσως το επιβατηγό οχηματαγωγό πλοίο «Απόλλων Εξπρές», η σωτήρια επέμβαση του οποίου απέτρεψε τον πιθανή τραγωδία.

Στο «ΖΕΥΣ 5», μήκος 32 μέτρων, επέβαιναν 20 Αμερικανοί συνταξιούχοι και 7μελές πλήρωμα. Η φωτιά εκδηλώθηκε στις 10 π.μ. στο μηχανοστάσιο και σε ελάχιστο χρόνο επεκτάθηκε και στον υπόλοιπο χώρο. Αμέσως, οι επιβάτες ειδοποιήθηκαν να φορέσουν τα σωσίβιά τους, ενώ έπεσαν στη θάλασσα οι σωσίβιες λέμβοι. Όπως δήλωσε ο ιδιοκτήτης της πλοιοκτήτριας εταιρίας «ΖΕΥΣ», κ. Τριαντάφυλλος Βενετόπουλος, η προσέλευση του «Απόλλων Εξπρές», που έλαβε το SOS, ήταν τόσο άμεση που δεν χρειάστηκε οι επιβάτες να μεταβιβαστούν στις λέμβους. Το επιβατηγό πλεύρισε δίπλα και με τη βοήθεια του πληρώματος επιβιβάστηκαν σ' αυτό οι Αμερικανοί τουρίστες.

Πλοίαρχος του «ΖΕΥΣ 5» είναι ο Δημήτρης Λειοσαίος και μηχανικός ο Γρηγόρης Μπίμας. «Θα συνεχίσουμε το ταξίδι μας χωρίς να αφήσουμε κα-

μιά αναποδιά να μας επηρεάσει», δήλωσε ο 65χρονος Tom Dowdell, επιβάτης της θαλαμηγού. Με εντυπωσιακή ψυχραιμία περιέγραψε το περιστατικό: «Οι περισσότεροι επιβάτες βρισκόμα-

σταν στο κεντρικό σαλόνι του πλοίου, όταν είδαμε τους καπνούς από το πίσω παράθυρο».

Όλοι οι επιβάτες τόνισαν πως «η επέμβαση του προσωπικού ήταν άμεση.

Χωρίς πανικό και με γρήγορες κινήσεις ειδοποιήθηκαν όλοι, εκτός από όσους βρίσκονταν στις καμπίνες τους, οι οποίοι οδηγήθηκαν στο τελευταίο κατάστρωμα.

Το πλοίο βυθίστηκε έξω από το λιμάνι της Ιου κα μαζί με αυτό και οι αποσκευές των επιβατών. Το πλήρωμα επιβιβάστηκε σε καΐκι, αφού είχε χαθεί και η τελευταία ελπίδα να περισωθεί το σκάφος από τις φλόγες.

Οι επιβάτες αποβιβάστηκαν χθες στις 8.00 μ.μ. στο λιμάνι του Πειραιά.

Τις επόμενες ημέρες έχουν προγραμματίσει να κάνουν το γύρο της Πελοποννήσου –αυτή τη φορά με πούλμαν– και όπως δήλωσαν, χαριτολογώντας– τίποτα δεν θα τους αλλάξει τα σχέδια.

Όπως δήλωσε ο πλοιοκτήτης του «ΖΕΥΣ 5», η εταιρία του θα μεριμνήσει για την επίλυση των προβλημάτων που θα τους δημιουργήσει η απώλεια των αποσκευών αλλά και των διαβατηρίων σε ορισμένους.

Το «ΖΕΥΣ 5» μετασκευάστηκε πέρυσι και πραγματοποιεί κρουαζιέρες σε ελληνικά νησιά. Στις 18 Απριλίου είχε αποπλεύσει από τη Μαρίνα Ζέας με προορισμό τα νησιά των Κυκλάδων. Ήταν κατασκευασμένο από μαόνι.

ΝΙΚΟΣ ΚΕΡΑΜΙΔΑΣ

Οι Αμερικανοί τουρίστες αντιμετώπισαν με ψυχραιμία το αναπάντεχο γεγονός και δήλωσαν ότι θα συνεχίσουν τις διακοπές τους.

True Soulmate: The Leica

Despite whatever film-loading failure occurred in Boston and Maine, Mom's deepest, most complex camera relationship was with that 1945 Leica II Dad brought home from Nuremberg. Almost as soon as she met Dad—when he began teaching at the private academy in 1949—the number of B&W square Brownie snapshots ebbed, and Mom began taking color slides. He didn't have a letterman sweater or class ring to give her;

he shared his camera. They were married a little over a year after meeting, and the Leica was part of the new family, recording their honeymoon, then the arrival and growth of 5 children.

The Brownie wasn't completely retired. I don't recall a family album of square B&W snapshots (there may have been one) but many B&W photos taken by Mom after starting her family were *returned* to her when my two grandmothers died and their photo albums distributed. So perhaps the Brownie was used to create photos Mom could mail and the recipient could see without a projector and screen. In the early 50s, slides were a method to take color photos without worrying about the much higher expense of color film, processing and printing.

> Kodachrome was originally mostly a transparency film—slides and motion pictures. Modern Kodachrome print film came along in 1961 and was improved again in 1974, just after Paul Simon's song "Kodachrome" was released.

Although it cost an expensive $200 in 1945 occupied Germany, the Leica was also a hybrid rangefinder—it could change lenses, but focusing and framing was not done *through* the lens. For that there was a viewfinder attachment that made the view look like what the zoom lens was seeing, only much smaller and hard to see. Choosing the correct aperture and speed were also difficult. Mom and the Leica constantly battled over exposure. Mom's slides could be dark to the

> Before 1961 the ASA speed of Kodachrome was between 8 and 10, meaning it was an insensitive film and required more light to create a "dense" image. In 1961 Kodachrome speed went up to 25 followed quickly in 1962 with Kodachrome 64.

point of silhouettes or washed to the point of ghosts, especially in difficult landscapes like the beach or snow.

One too dark, another too light but the shadows too dark. Mom threw away most of the worst offenders. Unless, like both of these, the main subject was still recognizable. In addition, when I scanned the slides, I tended to use photo software to try to repair poorly exposed images, so both of these are probably upgrades from the originals.

Focusing was another concept Mom and the Leica wrestled with. The focus ring was small, the view-finder tiny. And then there were those film sprockets. The Leica couldn't remind her to advance the film after taking a shot, and had no lock to prevent her from advancing the film twice. Long before the calamity in New England, film-advancement disputes with the Leica resulted in blank film or double exposures or something completely unexplainable.

And sometimes the Leica and Mom partnered for something exceptional.

The progeny produced by Mom and the Leica needed to be named and cared for. Perhaps she thought a metal "Kodaslide" storage system—manufactured in Rochester NY where Kodak was located—would work. But after the first one, the same year as her wedding, she switched to the AireQuipt magazine slide storage and projector attachment system. After going through a box of new slides (to cull the unredeemable duds), the slides would be labeled and loaded into a magazine.

In the naming, the slides carried on an evolving history. This is one reason I couldn't discard them after scanning. For example there was a time three was "the whole family," and the Christmas tree had to be moved outdoors so the Leica could produce the family holiday portrait.

Additionally Mom's editorial comments gave the slides personalities—or *Mom's* personality. The sun was in our eyes, the life jackets were swallowing us; Mom, never a *sad sack* herself, thought it was funny.

And did she remember when she also wore a white shirt to clean a fish as she took and captioned the photo of my brother after cleaning fish ... did she know she was creating symmetry, or a camera family tree?

Christopher & his catch

MADE IN U.S.A.

He cleaned them himself — Notice shirt!

MY FIRST ATTEMPT AT FISH CLEANING

The Leica stayed close to Mom for 30 years of her life, strapped to her body on her honeymoon and on Sierra hikes to 12,000 feet, while shepherding five kids through Washington DC on a scorching day in July and serving as the swim coach at Girl Scout camp. Beaches, mountains, boats, theme parks, zoos, hunting and fishing, flowers and sunsets, the Leica went along. But the Leica was inflexible about its limitations and Mom frustrated by an inability to work within those shortcomings. After the New England betrayal in 1971, the relationship had run its course.

In 2004, Mom cried when she opened her Christmas gift from Dad, a Sony digital camera kit. She may not have been sure why she wept. She was five years past a stroke that had impaired language-processing—a camera was more important to her than ever. Was that it? Or was there any residue of nostalgia for the one she'd loaded, focused, wound, wrangled and compromised with for thirty years? Of all the things I still have ... the projector, the magazines, the slides themselves ... the one thing no longer in her photography cache was the Leica itself.

June:
The Mother We Thought We Knew

June Cleaver didn't keep her house in perfect order. The prop man did it.
—Barbara Billingsly

An enchantment, a virtual bonding with June Cleaver grew over a span of roughly 93 weeks in 2015-16 when, daily with 6 a.m. coffee, I watched 15 minutes of *Leave it to Beaver*. That the 18+ months to briefly inhabit 234 episodes lay in the middle of three years when my mother languished and passed is not insignificant to both why the ritual was created and its impact, including the theme song becoming an ear worm that has lasted, now, going on five years. Not just the theme per-se, and not the jazz version that replaced the original when the kids got older, but the slow string rendition that always played at the epiphany and catharsis.

Leave it to Beaver aired from 1957 to 1963, depicting a family of four living in a lawn-and-sidewalk neighborhood in Mayfield, a fictional town in no particular state. Fittingly, my parents moved their growing family of 6 from residing on the grounds of a private academy on the Palos Verde Peninsula to a 1950s housing tract in San Diego where "Each house would have a lawn and a tree."[i] Development of this tract began in 1955, my family arrived there in 1959, and we left it (for what was then semi-rural San Diego County) in 1963—a pretty fair parallel to the Cleavers' life in Mayfield.

Plans for grid neighborhoods were being drawn before WWII, the earliest tracts began development in earnest in the mid 1940s, but the designation of first "mass produced" housing development is always given to the notorious Levittown, breaking ground in 1947. "Mass produced" means one developer building all the houses and then selling them. So, presumably, earlier tract developments sold the plotted sites and individuals had their own houses built.

Levittown was not infamous for mass-producing the houses, but for racial discrimination written into the ownership agreement of each sale. This became illegal after a pair of 1947 and 1948 Supreme Court rulings that prohibited local governments from enforcing racially restrictive covenants that had regularly been a clause in property deeds. "Ignoring the law of the land, however, Levitt continued adhering to its racial bar."[ii] As for neighborhood tracts in California, they should have eliminated contractual racial restrictions in 1948, but the state and local real estate boards, instigators of restrictive covenants in the early 1900s, continued to encourage racial restrictions written into property deeds, some of which are still found in those deeds now.[iii] While technically unenforceable, implementation was purportedly taken up by sales people in new housing developments, warning minority buyers it was not in their best interest to move into these neighborhoods. Urban legend has it that a development in Los Angeles County, five years older than the one my parents chose in San Diego, asked Italian-American buyers to prove they were not Mexican.

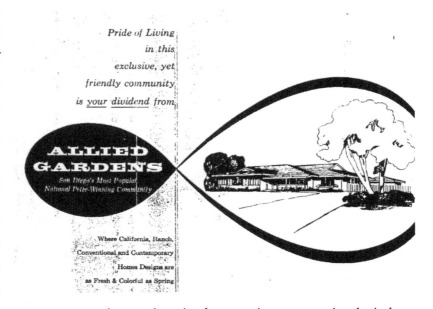

Meanwhile in Hollywood, the fabricating of fictious 1957 Mayfield and the family living there included a few subtle instances of moderately progressive ideas, including in 1957 a fleeting view of the top of a toilet tank (not the seat), the first view of a toilet on television; a 1958 story involving a Spanish-speaking friend named Chuey (note: not Mexican, the boy's father was a diplomat from South America; one wonders why a diplomat would be located in Mayfield); and a 1960 episode that will come into play later.

Beaver seemed about 5 or 6 years old in the first (1957) season, but the show itself clarified he was 7 going on 8. Either I am not good at estimating a child's age or the show wrote Beaver's earliest childhood scenes to stay babyish longer. I, however, was 1-year-old and not, in any stretch, Beaver's age. And by the time I first watched the show in re-runs, I might have been 12, so while his constant attire in blue jeans attracted my fashion sensibility, he was not ever an emblematic peer. I don't remember watching the show in the late 60s—i.e. my dad actually choosing that channel and letting us watch it—but my recall suggests I did see one particular episode when Beaver's voice had already changed and Wally was having a "teenage party" with dancing, boys wearing suits and girls full-skirted dresses, and nothing looked like the world I lived in or the teenaged life I might soon be entering. It's possible I saw that episode as a first-run in 1963, when "teenagers," and not housewives, were my baleful fascination.

Nearing adulthood in the 70s, in an earlier era of watching the show's re-run syndication, I would not have been very aware of June except to have the usual, now stock, response that she was a stereotype of something that never existed, wearing dresses, heels and pearls as she cleaned house and cooked. Turns out Barbara Billingsly mandated that her skirt length not be low mid-thigh nor above the knee.[iv] She didn't

specify who mandated she wear only dresses and skirts, but it's interesting how it was considered groundbreaking when Mary Tyler Moore wore "capris" as a wife on *The Dick Van Dyke Show* nine years later in 1966. (June did not get forerunner credit even though she did wear "trousers" herself on at least one episode where she—not convincingly in my experience—was gardening. Billingsly did wonder, in a 2003 interview, why they didn't allow her to wear pants more often.) The heels were foisted upon Billingsly, who'd begun the show in casual flats, because the two child actors were growing quickly, and producers wanted June to remain taller than her sons. And the famous pearls: This piece of wardrobe was added by Billingsly in collaboration with production, because

the hollow of her throat was pronounced and caused a shadow which appeared, on TV, like a large hole in her neck.[v]

There was no further occasion for me to ponder June until her iconic appearance on *Airplane* in 1980, when she volunteers, "excuse me, I speak Jive," and proceeds to "translate" a form of Black vernacular for the perplexed stewardess—probably still, at the time, called a *stewardess*, just as African American Vernacular English (AAVE) was called *jive*. The joke not just that an older white woman is able to "speak jive" with young African American men, but that the woman is, in fact, *June Cleaver*, the archetype American housewife, which may have never existed in actuality. The underlying racist "gag" here is that the movie's writers were, in fact, *denigrating* so-called "jive." They invented the vernacular used in the movie precisely to make it gibberish. Before Billingsly stepped up to translate (and speak it herself), the movie ran subtitles for what the two men were saying, to deepen both the irony of the gender-icon (Billingsly) and the racism-of-the-era "joke."[vi] At the time, I had no idea the "jive" in the movie was not AAVE (formerly called Ebonics). For me the intended irony of having June Cleaver be the jive translator hit its mark.

Three years later (1983) CBS tapped into the earliest era of Baby Boomer nostalgia—the 2nd half of the Boomers might be in the 2nd phase of grad school, caught between childhood and starting life—with a TV movie, *Still the Beaver*, starring both boys now as men, and Barbara Billingsly still their mother. Beaver had become (as could have been predicted by how many times Wally called him *a goof*), a fuck-up, divorced and living with his mom. When June is "worried about the Beaver," she goes to Ward's grave to talk to him. [Hugh Beaumont had died in 1982; research has not answered whether the 1983 movie was in production yet and thus had to be re-written.]

As a graduate student in Brooklyn, I watched the movie on a 13-inch B&W TV I'd bought and lugged on a bus back to the bedroom I rented in Flatbush. Beaver's continual ineffectiveness in life and doleful expressions didn't impress me as much as June's earnest conversations with her dead husband. Three-thousand miles away from my parents, I was in an emerging awareness that there had not been and possibly never would be life-lesson dialogues with either my father or mother, and that moving back home for any reason would produce nothing but a milieu of disgust and contempt. This doesn't mean I necessarily wished my camp-counselor, swimming-coach, girl-scout-leader Mom was more like June Cleaver.

Sometimes Mom wore dresses, sometimes jeans, sometimes shorts, sometimes a bathing suit, sometimes (after they were invented) a pantsuit. No makeup except lipstick. No pearls, unless fake ones, and no hairdresser until she was adding a paycheck to the family finances. That wasn't until after her youngest was in kindergarten and she went back to college for 4 or 5 years (one class a semester at first) to get a teaching credential, then began work teaching 4th grade. Yes, we had to wash for dinner and sit all together at a dining room table; no, we didn't stay in our rooms (dealing with a goof-up that would soon be discovered) until food was ready to eat. Yes, she vacuumed, did laundry and dusted furniture; no, she didn't do it alone in the background of our "important" lives. Yes, we were primarily aware of our own daily problems, worries and social negotiations, with no notion of hers; no, it wasn't true that she never cried within our hearing.

In the evening when she was tired—and it is only now that I know how tired—if we asked her to play a boardgame, she usually would. Take a dozen 11-year-olds on a campout, or roller skating, or a dozen 7-year-olds on a field trip: yes, she would. Fish

a Sierra stream, shoot and clean a dove, mold a ceramic nude, get the roller-coaster to stop just to remove her own screaming child: yes, she did. I didn't need June Cleaver.

Yet, during my most recent foray into *Leave it to Beaver*, before dawn with breakfast, June Cleaver captured my admiration in a way that elevated her (almost) to my mother's status. And yes, they both made mistakes.

By February 1961 Beaver was going through pre-adolescence. His voice was changing and he might have become tall enough that June's heels no longer did their job, so direction began using a method where June might either be seated or standing on the first step of the stairway when she and Beaver spoke. Written into the storyline for "Nobody Loves Me," Beaver gets plenty of overly obvious plot-complicating messages, both direct and indirect, that he was formerly cute but now has become grubby, awkward, ugly, and unlovable. When June and Ward become aware of Beaver's misery (as so frequently happens, Wally gives them parenting advice), they go to Beaver and tell him one of those stories about "a friend and his son," and how parents will always love their children but later, as their children grow, they even come to respect them. The slow string-orchestra version of the theme song will play here.

Mom didn't have the opportunity to play a scene like this because she never knew when or how I was introduced to my own pulsating, gross inelegance; she was too busy raising five children with ages spanning 10 years. One complicating factor for me was that while my height never exceeded 5-feet, I did become taller than my next-older sister. By junior high, certainly in high school, I felt monstrous to her dainty. Overlapping this growth era, there was a period of many years when Mom would have the same petite next-elder sister give violin concerts for relatives during visits while the rest of us struggled with the obvious status of undistinguished bystander.

But way before that evidence of my inconsequence, Mom had two children younger than me who had slipped into the "cute" phase as I slipped out. One evening she settled onto the sofa with her three younger children to read us a story. She only had two sides to her. Was one little brother on one side and the other on her lap, giving me her remaining side? That part I don't recall. What I do remember is her elbow pushing me away, and her voice, "don't lean on me, you're too heavy."

In 1960 the series aired a show called "Larry's Club." This is a story too many of us may recognize, from both sides of the story's conflict. The boys Beaver's age have formed a secret club. Beaver joined, but then was told that this club would be excluding Beaver's friend Larry Mondello because the club was only for "neat guys." In fact, as Whitey says (and was it an accident *Whitey* was chosen to say this?), "the only reason to have a club is so you can keep other guys out." Naturally hurt, Larry figures out his own way to respond: he tells Beaver *he* had an even more secret club. Larry's club has armbands and even "a secret hood."

"Must be a real neat club to have hoods and everything," Beaver exclaims. Then Larry adds that the paper bag hoods are only temporary until they get their *velvet* hoods. (Certain parts of the KKK uniform are made of velvet.) The club would also wear blue sweaters (throwing us off the KKK trail) and have secret meetings in graveyards. But Larry doesn't think *The Fiends* (*friends* without the r) will let Beaver join, but maybe he can attend a special meeting, under certain conditions: Beaver will have to be blindfolded to attend the secret acceptance meeting. Larry carries off the whole fabricated club meeting and vote until Beaver, tearing off the blindfold, discovers that Larry's club is a ruse.

Again in this instance, my mom and June resolve the problem in different ways. My sixth grade class was dividing into groups to create, write and perform puppet shows. The groups were all determined by the 11-year-olds. Memory doesn't help me know why I was excluded from every group. I do recall the exclusion was of the "No, not you" variety that Larry experienced, except girl-style with the silent-treatment. It was a rare instance (and maybe the last one) when I told Mom my dilemma. She must have elicited from me the name of another girl who had been excluded; we knew her from Girl Scouts. Mom picked up the girl, brought her home, she had dinner with us, and the other girl and I, in a group of two, fabricated hand puppets and a cardboard stage. Decades later, after my first memoir was published, that girl—who'd been raised by a single mother working full time and knew my mom as her Girl Scout leader and—

told me she always pictured my childhood home as one where the mom was regularly organizing crafts, games and activities. I've remembered this incident because of the hurt, and the embarrassment of my puppet stage being the smallest (and the only one not painted "psychedelic"), and because my Mom responded proactively, but not because there was a lesson imparted. In fact, I was one of the "mean girls" at some point that same year.

I and several others wrote and shared "Debbie Books"—folded-together pamphlets with lists of unkind untruths about a girl in our class. If my 6th grade teacher had discovered and rebuked our meanness and then told our parents … there *is* a story my mother could have told me then:

Physical education majors at Sargent College were required to take summer activity courses at a remote site in New Hampshire—sailing, canoeing, horseback riding, swimming, field sports. The all-girls college camp's facilities included kiosks with cots for sleeping bags. The summer before senior year, 1945, Mom's group was worried; there were two African American girls in their class, and they wanted the whole group to stay together in the kiosk, but the administration felt the Black girls "would be more comfortable" sleeping by themselves in another location. These girls swam in the same pools, played team sports together, and dressed in the same locker rooms. In Mom's story, she was the one who went to the dean to explain that the senior class wanted to remain together, and the dean (therefore?) allowed integrated housing for the summer camp of 1945. Mom's telling was without surprise that the dean would relent. I don't know what the group would have done if he hadn't. One hint: among my mother's papers, there were saved news articles about the same group of phys. Ed. majors

forming a strike when the merger with Boston University threatened to change the name of their college, and they won that standoff to keep its original name. But there is no artifact evidence of their venture into demands for civil rights. It's left to conjecture whether or not they would have moved on to some form of protest if the dean had said no to non-segregated camp housing.

Mom didn't find a reason to tell me how she'd argued against segregated housing until I was writing my first memoir and I was asking questions about her college years. She never had the opportunity to react to my most extreme venture into schoolyard cruelty (now called bullying), but I wonder if she would have made the connection I'm making now. The one Ward didn't, but June did, eventually make.

When June and Ward discover Beaver's experience with exclusive clubs (again, Wally has the inside dope), June says, "I don't like the idea of boys Beaver's age forming clubs to keep other boys out." Ward agrees but doesn't "want to make a lecture out of it." He "*could* level with him, but that sounds so corny." What sounds corny, Ward? Who wrote that line? And the qualifier of "boys Beaver's age" for June's line?

But it turns out, Beaver was attuned to metaphor. Ward tells him not a personal story from his life, but a parable about a village of friendly people who all worked together. Then a sub-group decided to build a castle, and the castle is constructed to keep other people out. Other groups followed and built castles, until there were six castles. The people in one castle wouldn't talk to the others. They wouldn't work together or help each other. When an invader came, because the people were so suspicious of each other, the invader was able to capture all six castles, "one by one."

Poland, Belgium, Austria, Norway, Denmark, France … Actually there were more than six.

Beaver catches on quickly. "Are those castles like clubs?" And when his father says yes, Beaver quotes good-old Whitey: "Whitey says the only reason to have a club is so you can keep other guys out."

"When people divide up into groups just to hurt others, sooner or later they're going to end up like those people in the castles." Was Ward (through the writers) more consciously thinking of the run-up to World War II, and not minorities in the U.S. facing segregation? Seems likely. So it was up to June to nail it.

After Ward returns downstairs, June asks, "Did you explain about clubs?"

"No … castles." Not prevalent in North American segregation, but there were plenty of castles in pre-WWII Europe. Conveniently, also a staple of children's literature. Ward explains, "How else to get a little guy's interest?"

The couple is standing close, but not touching, and Ward then muses, "I wonder, what do people who live in castles tell their children?"

What a strange line to write. Unless the two actors adlibbed. That's what I'd like to believe. Because June—or Barbara Billingsly—replied, "Probably stories about Levittown."

Notes

[i] https://anderstomlinson.com/garden-2/low-water-garden/welcome-to-allied-gardens/

[ii] http://ushistoryscene.com/article/levittown/

[iii] Kim, Cristina, "How Discriminatory Covenants Shaped San Diego Homeownership," KPBS, Nov. 17, 2021

[iv] https://www.latimes.com/archives/la-xpm-2003-feb-10-et-quintanilla10-story.html

[v] ibid

[vi] https://movies.stackexchange.com/questions/11208/translating-the-jive-dialogue

Someone Said No

Among the ways I am fortunate: I am allowed to live mostly far removed from "the base"—the racists, the flat-earthers, the climate-change deniers, the Fixed News watchers, all the Antis (reproductive choice, LGBTQ rights, masks and vaccines, the Affordable Health Care Act, etc.). Currently, my progressive, educated milieu is a culture trying to look race issues and concepts squarely in the eye. Involuntary white-guilt aside, I have struggled with foibles like: learning my African American students' names easily but struggling to correctly pin the Vanessas, Kathryns, Jasons and Ryans; or teasingly calling a student *Ivan the Great* before realizing his (Latino) name is pronounced Ē-Vón, not Eyé-van; or being (tacitly) startled upon learning an African American student was home-schooled, even though everything else about him made sense in that context. Yet I hadn't been moved to much exploration of race in my universe.

Until the photo of my mother in blackface was discovered.

For the almost 75 years of her post-adolescence, Mom vivaciously relished marriage, children, friends, family-events, travel, food, games and athletics, camping, hiking, hunting, fishing, canning, crocheting, bridge parties, watercolor classes. It becomes a typical, even clichéd obituary. But when obituary-writing landed on my desk, the list was already too crowded to also include: declining her father's gender-groundbreaking offer to give her his dental practice because she would rather do athletics; majoring in phys-ed at an all-female college in the early 1940s with no means of turning college into an "MRS degree"; protesting her college's policy of housing an African American student separately during required summer athletics, or (just a few years later at her first post-college job) participating in a blackface event. Of course the latter would never suit an epitaph.

Who Was She Before She Was *Mom*?

At some point in the second half of the nineties, at the first stirring to write about my mother's life, I interviewed her about what it was like to major in physical education in the War years, to be at a women's college when most young men her age were in in the military. I wanted to know about her academics and her social life, especially dating. (As far as we know, our parents never had any previous relationships before each other.) Despite my fanatical record-keeping and ambition to control chaos, the notes from the interview haven't been located because the current pandemic has prohibited searching boxes of archives located elsewhere. Yet I've managed to retain in memory several amazing details (context, analysis and conjectures are mine):

That: In an era when a class at dental college might have one female student, if any, (even by 1972 girls were still being told "you'll take the place of a man"), Mom's father offered his youngest child the idea of going to dental school and taking over his practice. Her reason for declining the offer: not that she wanted to get married and have children (which clearly she did) but that she had more interest in sports and wanted to pursue a BS in physical education.

That: The War Years were, as she remembered, "a world of women." She claimed no interest in the "90 day wonders"—young men attending officers training at nearby colleges who would be gone three months or less after any acquaintance began.

That: Empowerment of women in the workforce trickled down to teenagers and young women gaining a sense of independence beyond being an income-earner. There was a threatened strike to keep the name of their college from changing, generating this commentary (which *she* clipped and taped to a file card in 1944).

> Boston University, under duress, agrees that alumnae of that college may call it Sargent. This shows what a college education does for determined girls, especially if it includes jujitsu.

Founded in 1881 as Sargent School of Physical Training, then acquired by Boston University in 1929 and accredited as a college, the school offered college degrees in physical education and physical therapy. In 1944, Boston University sought to change the name from Boston University Sargent College of Physical Education to Boston University College of Physical Education. The students rallied, petitioned, protested, threatened a strike, until the proposed name-change reached compromise. The school would be Boston University College of Physical Education for Women Sargent College.

The administration's compromise to avoid the "strike" actually made the name worse than leaving it as it was.

NO OTHER NAME COULD BE AS SWEET to students Martha Kloo (left) of West Hartford, Conn., and Eleanor Young of Newton Centre, as they learned that Sargent College would officially keep its name, after a week's protest to Boston University.

I already knew this was not the only petition raised by the students in the 1940s. But it was the one that merited newspaper coverage.

The other appeal, not protected in any brittle yellowed news clipping, involved segregation: [Edited from my first memoir where I initially represented the event.]

As [summer athletic] camp approached before her senior year, my mother and her friends were a little worried. Two girls in my mother's class were Black, and in 1945 at Sargent College the Black girls—girls who attended the same classes, swam in the same pool, dressed in the same locker-room, played on the same teams—were housed separately. My mother's group wanted to stay together, so she and a friend went to the dean to request permission for the Black girls to bunk in their kiosk. The dean, my mother remembers, gave the (now familiar) rationale for the school's policy, always couched in terms of what was best for "*them*"—that "*they*" would be much more comfortable if housed separately. No, my mother explained to the dean, they want to be with us. No strikes, no sit-ins or protests were needed... The dean relented, and Sargent's segregated housing policy was suspended ...

Now freshly discovered artifacts further inflame the ache that seeks to reconstruct my parents' lives after it's too late to hear their narratives or ask further questions: Who were the two African American young women? Was it really senior year? Were they really *friends*? Who *was* Miss Sepia 1944?

Who Was Miss Sepia 1944? (And why does it matter?)

From a defunct minor city newspaper, a single clipping, found among my mother's letters and other paper keepsakes. Unfortunately the forensic chain-of-possession documentation failed—I never noted the exact location in which I found it and what else was beside it. The clipping is dated 1944, Mom's sophomore year of college. The clipping's photo subject: the contestants for the 1944 Miss Sepia America Beauty and Talent Contest of greater Boston. Crosschecking names with Mom's college yearbooks, only one matched: Gwendolyn Freeman. She attended college the same four years that Mom did. When Miss Freeman's photo appeared in *The Boston Traveler*, Mom clipped and saved it. There is no follow-up clipping giving the results of the contest. "Final

BOSTON TRAVELER, FRIDAY, APRIL 7, 1944

BEAUTIES who registered in the Sepia American Beauty and Talent Contest launched this week in Boston to select the outstanding Negro beauty in the country and crown her the Sepia Miss America are, left to right: Patricia Rainey, Dorchester; Chirlaine J. Dupree, Boston; Marilyn Roberts, Roxbury; Mae Yates, Roxbury, and Gwendolyn Freeman, Boston. The final eliminations will be held in June in Chicago.

eliminations" were to have been held in Chicago that summer of '44. The summer 1944 issue of *The Crisis*—founded by W.E.B. Du Bois, quarterly magazine of the NAACP—featured a one-page spread showing the "Lovely Lassies in the Sepia Miss America Contest." *The Crisis* caption says the five featured girls were the contestants from Greater Boston, and that The Sepia Miss America Committee of Boston had launched plans for a "nationwide series of contests to select the outstanding Negro beauty."

July, 1944 221

LOVELY LASSIES IN THE SEPIA MISS AMERICA CONTEST

The five gorgeous lassies at the top (left to right) are Priscilla Wichner, Charlaine J. Dupree, who has already won a dramatic scholarship to Hollywood's leading workshop for the screen, Eleanor Tabor, Gloria Eaves, and Dorothy Bruce, contestants from Greater Boston, Mass. Review (left to right): Dorothy Bruce, Charlaine J. Dupree, and Eleanor Tabor. The Sepia Miss America Committee of Boston, Mass., has launched plans for a nationwide series of contests to select the outstanding Negro beauty in the country and crown her Miss Sepia America. The contest will continue through the fall.

Only one name in *The Crisis* spread of Boston contestants is also listed in *The Traveler's* photo caption of those who had just registered for the Boston contest. Deduction: Mom's classmate Gwendolyn Freeman didn't make the final cut for the Boston Miss Sepia contest. Charlaine DuPree, named in both articles, was also featured on the front page of *The Ohio State News* (an African American newspaper published 1935-52), but the caption only indicates Miss. Dupree was one of the first contestants to enter (thus she's also in the *Traveler* photo) and doesn't give any update on the contest results. From there, not only the 1944 results, but the history of Miss Sepia America, or Sepia Miss America, is muddled at best. As is much of what I apparently don't know about my mother.

Ninety-seven years after Canada began observing "Emancipation Day," the 1931 festival organizer, Walt Perry, expanded festivities to four days and included a parade, fair rides, musical performances, skill demonstrations, and a beauty contest called "Miss Sepia." No (internet) evidence of any Miss Sepia contest hits again until 1939 when actor/producer Eddie Green's Sepia-Art Pictures Company released the film *What Goes Up*, purportedly including an actress discovered in a "Miss Sepia New Jersey" contest at New York's Rockland Palace. Then a search hit in 1940: a publicity sheet for Eddie Green's film *One Round Jones*—posted online by Green's daughter Elva who explains the cast includes Miss Sepia America 1940, "crowned at the World's Fair."

The Boston area Miss Sepia America Beauty and Talent Contest of 1944 is the next hit, featuring only the pictorial page in *The Boston Traveler* (April 1944) and *The Crisis* (July 1944), neither of which ever announces a contest winner.

A tumblr account called "oldshowbiz" posted another item about Eddie Green and his Miss Sepia contest of 1940, but the tumblr post cut-in the same 1944 pictorial page from *The Crisis* as though those were the finalists in Green's 1940 contest.

Then a Philadelphia Facebook group takes credit for starting the Miss Sepia Beauty Pageant. "Established in 1945 in Philadelphia by Grayce Clementine Nottage and her sister Ruth, the Miss Sepia beauty pageant was open to single black girls between the ages of 17 and 24 who were high school seniors or graduates."

The last hit is back in *The Crisis* in 1948, and only in a tiny advertisement for The Carver School of Business in Philadelphia (long defunct), a sentence offering *Instruction and personality development given by Gwen Schooh, Director of the Miss Sepia Contest.*

Enigmatic that the trail ends with another name of Gwen(dolyn). But nothing answers why Mom saved that 1944 clipping of Boston contest entrants.

Who Was Going to be Housed Separately ... and When?

Start with *Who*. In 1942-43 there were 112 names of freshmen in the Sargent College yearbook. There were only photos of 36, and those captioned only with first names or nicknames. Mom was *Squeaky*, a nickname she banished in the 70s when Squeaky Frome attempted an assassination of President Ford. Among the 36 thumbnail faces in B&W, there is one girl, with no nickname but a complete first name, *Jacqueline*, who is African

American. The list of all 112 names identifies her as Jacqueline Jefferson of Philadelphia.

In 1943-44, Mom's sophomore yearbook gives 110 names, with only 68 having a small photo with a first-name or nickname. None are Jacqueline or Jackie, none of the photos suggests any race other than Caucasian. Jacqueline Jefferson *is* among the complete list of names.

The yearbook from 1944-45 lists 102 names of juniors, and now has 74 photos of them, but the photos are not captioned at all. In the 74 photos, there is one African American young woman, astride what seems to be a log bridge. In the club photos—captioned only for the activity—an African American young woman appears in the Dance Club. It's possible the thumbnail-size log photo is the same person as the dance club member. But also possible that it's not. What is clear is that Jacqueline Jefferson's name no longer appears in the class list.

Senior year, 1945-46, the yearbook put two or three larger photos on each page for the seniors. There are no captions, only hand-drawn figures depicting an activity—sketched in Mom's unmistakable style. Mom's illustration is an archer. The young woman above Mom on the page is African American, and her drawing is a dancer. This photo is clear enough to show she is the same person as the dance club member in the junior year annual. On other senior pages in the yearbook, the photos do not have printed names but have the students' signatures *on* their photos, yet on Mom's page the signatures are too light to read. It is also clear the other photos/signatures come in alphabetical order. In the junior yearbook's printed class list, Mom (Elinore Young) is the last name. The name just before hers was Margaret Truth Wooten. Going back to the earliest yearbooks, Ms. Wooten's name appears in all four of Mom's yearbooks. As a sophomore, she signed beside her printed name on the list of students: *Remember all the laughs we had in JK6 and also in biology.*

Another name appears in all four yearbooks: Gwendolyn Freeman.

Mom's narration of "two girls" who were going to be housed separately appears accurate. While for two of Mom's college years, there were at least three African American students, in her last two years there were only two. The senior class group portrait confirms this.

Left: Compare Gwendolyn in the senior group with Gwendolyn in the *Boston Traveler* clipping (p. 60).
Center: Margaret Wooten – clearly the same person as the portrait on the right.
Right: Margaret Wooten's faint signature near her collar shows up with photo enlargement and enhancement.

So if Mom's memory of lobbying the dean to not separately house *two* Black girls was accurate, does that also make it accurate that she remembered it as her senior year? That would put this request after the successful student protest against changing the name of their school, the lesson in "what a college education does for determined girls." And yet …

In Margaret Wooten's sophomore yearbook signature, she "remembers the laughs" in JK6 and biology. Mom's transcript shows biology in fall of her freshman year. So the "laughs" she and Margaret shared started there. What about *JK6*? At the required sessions of summer camp—one in June and another in September, where the students participated in outdoor team sports, swimming, boating, sailing, and other activities that couldn't be accomplished during winter in Boston—they slept in *kiosks*. Mom recalled them as "bungs" short for bungalow. Her oral story about asking that the Black girls be allowed to sleep with the rest of their class specifically referenced the "senior bung." Margaret's yearbook inscription remembered JK6, and, back in the freshman yearbook, another girl signed, recalling their fun in EK2. This verifies that the initials do reference a camp kiosk; reveals that incoming freshmen did one summer stint at the athletics camp before their first fall semester; and thirdly confirms that Margaret's reference to JK6 was, in fact, a (not segregated) camp kiosk before their sophomore year, in 1943.

Most is also corroborated with photos in Mom's personal album, including "the

gang from K2" dated June 1944 (sophomore year). No photo in her album *identifies* a "K6," which would have been in the summer of 1943 where Mom's "gang" would have included Margaret Wooten. Mom had no photos of kiosk-life in 1943, nor any photos of life in the "senior bung" in 1945. But in the sophomore (43-44) yearbook there's a photo of

girls with luggage, waiting outside the kiosks. It's evident an African American girl was in the group staying in *this* kiosk.

The senior yearbook had no typeset words. Typesetting for a yearbook would have been, in the 1940s (in fact *until* the 1960s), an outside service, would cost a fair amount, and would increase the price of a yearbook. So the staff of the senior yearbook (Mom included) had to plan ahead. When they wanted words, they endeavored to get them into the photographs in other ways: each senior signed her photo, groups of girls

held signs, or photographs were arranged to form words. Another way they included words was in line drawings, using handwritten words. The yearbook includes a 2-page spread of a hand-drawn map of the summer athletic camp

facility, with (hand) cut-out photos added. (Mom is the tunic-wearing field hockey player right of center.)

The map reveals "The Senior Bung," "The Junior Bung," and at least fourteen smaller cabins, referred as kiosks. As mentioned, Mom had no photo of K6 from 1943, but a yearbook photo from Sept 1944 possibly shows Margaret Wooten (middle right; Mom on far left).

If, as it appears, Margaret Wooten was housed in a kiosk with Mom in sophomore year 1943, was *that* the year the students organized to end segregated housing?

But there are two further elements to consider: First, the dean to whom the appeal was made. The dean of Sargent College had remained the same man (of course) from before Mom's freshman year until August 1, 1945, which would have been *before* her September 1945 senior year session of athletic camp. And second, my own narrative, based on how Mom told me this story in the '90s: that she and her friends "were worried as the athletic camp approached before their senior year." Why were they worried *then*? What was different to cause worry after 3-1/2 years? Was it that the new dean, who began in August, was suggesting segregated housing for the September camp session?

Rather than question my mother's memory that she made an entreaty to the dean in her *senior* year; rather than assume that it took *until* 1945 for the seniors at Sargent college to decide they would galvanize a movement to stop the practice of housing the African American girls separately; it actually seems more credible that in 1945 the college (or *someone*) had wanted to *start* housing those girls separately. And the students in the senior class said no.

Margaret Wooten was not one of the classmates Mom stayed in touch with after college. Margaret's obituary (2010) was entirely photographs of her as an older woman, with her children and grandchildren, but—much like her college yearbooks—no text to summarize where her life had gone after college. In the 1946 Boston University yearbook (different than the textless Sargent College yearbook), Margaret signed "remember how we used to take <u>notes</u> in Mrs. G—'s class." (An insinuation they had, instead of taking academic notes, *passed* notes?) But no suggestion they should stay in touch. And for Gwendolyn Freeman—with no unique middle name like Margaret's "Truth"—there has not been a digital search that yielded anything about her, not even the Miss Sepia contestants photo from *The Boston Traveler*. The reference to a Gwen Schooh who was director of the Miss Sepia contest and coached contestants at an African American School of Business in Philadelphia, likewise left no trail I could follow to see if they were the same person.

Moving West, Still Not Finished Becoming

Upon graduation, Mom vaulted across the country, going from a racially troubled city's public university—one that had a written policy denying racial barriers—to a private academy in supposedly progressive Southern California.

> "The time is at hand, when every Christian country will demand that its highest and best educational appliances, organized in its universities, be made available to all comers, without respect to creed or race or sex."
> —Boston University President William Fairfield Warren, 1874

The bounce from Boston to Southern California actually took longer than a week and was spanned by car, accompanied by her parents and an aunt and uncle, zig-zagging north to Niagara falls, angling south through the Midwest, through some national parks in the West, before arriving at Chadwick Seaside Academy where she'd been offered a job as girls physical education teacher for K-12.

Mom's first 20 years of life do reek of privilege. Her dentist father often took payment in goods during the depression, but still, all three of her older siblings went to college, and she was a college educated woman during the War Years. Getting her job at the boarding school had a tint of nepotism as it had been offered due to her Harvard educated brother's relationship with a member of the school's board. The pay was low but included room-and-board, and her job included filling in at the front desk during the receptionist's lunch hour, and (at 21-years-old) sitting at the "parent's" place at family-style meals in the dining hall.

For three years as a single young woman, then for two more years after meeting my father but before she was married, she lived on campus. The first three years, as she had through college, she ravenously took photos and kept steadily-growing-less-elaborate photo albums, depicting her students' activities, plus social or noteworthy occasions at the school. Her means of communicating with her own mother was all in letters, but she developed the habit of including photographs to illustrate her narratives. Those albums end after 1949. At that point she may have moved to color slides (developing a color slide was much cheaper than a color print in the 1950s), and any B&W photos taken at Chadwick School that I have gathered were likely taken by someone else.

When, married, Mom returned to Chadwick in 1954 with her two toddlers, she taught only part time for parts of the next five years. In the headmistress's self-published history of Chadwick school, *A Dipperful of Humanity*, the author skips from Mom's predecessor to the teacher/coach who followed her without any mention of Mom. She was erased.

In telling the story of how my parents met at Chadwick School, my impulse has always been to tell from my father's experience: After his immigrant parents lost everything in the depression, he'd quit school and the whole family moved to California, selling trinkets at state fairs along the way. In San Pedro, California, Dad finally resumed 9th grade, two years older than his classmates, plus he worked part time as a janitor for the nascent Chadwick School in their temporary location. From there the formula was quid-pro-quo: the school needed state accreditation, for that they possibly needed a graduate who could meet qualifications for a Calif public university. The handful of kids who would be the first graduating class were only inclined toward private colleges, so the headmistress offered her part-time janitor the opportunity to attend her school for his final two years of high school. He boarded there when the school moved to its permanent location on the Palos Verdes Peninsula, then the Chadwick board partially paid his way to University of California. The War interrupted his education, but after he returned and finished (on the G.I. Bill), Chadwick School hired him in 1949 to teach chemistry. So he was a new teacher in Mom's fourth year. By 1951 they had married, left Chadwick for a period of about 3 years and had their first 2 children. He tacked on a master's degree, taught science in public schools, then [for reasons I can only speculate] returned his family to Chadwick, living on about $250 a month in a tiny stucco bungalow on the Chadwick property, adding two more children … all while mingling with and educating the children of enormously wealthy movie stars, musicians and business tycoons.

By the time my parents decided to move their growing family away from the milieu of uber-affluence (which we would now call the 1%)—with the prime reason being they didn't want "it" to be an influence (or pressure) on their children—Mom had become *Mom*, her experiences as a single woman would be of no interest to her offspring's perceptions for many decades.

In 1947, the faculty basketball team (also) seemed to have dressed in costume(s). Were they all attempting to replicate "gypsy" attire, or had each member decided on a separate get-up? All that's knowable (to me) is Mom in the lower right, and that there's a man (the headmaster) in a dress who, in other photos, seems to be the referee. The action shots on the same page show the student team in standard phys ed. uniforms. Apparently the student-vs-teacher basketball

game was a traditional occasion for frivolity, if not discernment.

The blackface faculty basketball photograph was not in one of Mom's Chadwick School photo albums. It was not included in Chadwick yearbooks. My sister found it in a folder in Mom's desk drawer when the house was being cleared out to sell in 2018, and that's when any of us first saw it. The few other photos in the same folder contained photos of Mom on the Chadwick campus, Mom on a California beach, and one of Mom sailing in New England in college. All of them, except the basketball team, were duplicates of other photos from her college or Chadwick albums, which would explain why those were not in albums. The folder betrayed no information as to the basketball photo's date nor why it was in a folder instead of in an album. For my untrained archive-forensic brain, however, hints emerge from both the front and the back (front is cropped and enlarged).

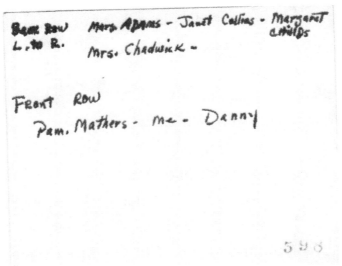

Since Mom and Dad temporarily left Chadwick after June 1951, the photo dates before that. The size, paper-quality and style/location of the number stamped on the back make this photo *precisely* comparable to a series of loose B&W photos of Chadwick (photographer unknown) in my collection that date around 1950-51.

That Mom would caption the photo with (mostly) first *and* last names but not put it into her album suggests this might be one she sent to her mother in a letter. Then, decades later when her mother's possessions were divided, most of those photos came back, some in hodge-podge albums, some separately. It's too easy to say Mom stashed it in a desk out of embarrassment; more likely because her old albums were somewhere in a cupboard above her closet and she had no time to update them.

Among the names written on the back, Janet Collins was the 6th grade teacher and elementary school principal. One memory of her in the headmistress's history says she shared her "vivid recollections from Haiti." Three of the others are from the business office, the educational office, and the headmistress herself, who claimed her school "represented a wide diversity of races, religions, and riches."

Mom is center front. Beside her is the most impactful detail *after* the shock of the greasepaint: the young woman, lower-right, who did not go along. The identification on the back gives her name: Danny. For reasons unknown, she is the only one with no last name given; perhaps Mom had already introduced Danny to her mother in a letter. Her full name was Virginia Daniels. She taught English and literature from 1943 to 1970 and was in a life-relationship with a female teacher who was not participating on the faculty basketball team; the two of them commonly identified with an ampersand, *Gin-&-Danny*. Their story will continue later. For now, all the photograph says of them, of any of them, is that this time Mom said yes, but someone—maybe two someones—did say no.

Getting Their Stories Straight

How could there even have been, in my native (and presumably eternally progressive) Southern California, a blackface event for my mother to agree to participate in? And at Chadwick Seaside Academy in Palos Verdes, the faculty basketball team of 1950 wasn't the only occasion—two other blackface incidents are shown in the school's 1948 yearbook.

Years later, our parents said they chose to remove us from the influences and peer-groups found at the private boarding academy where they lived and taught, where the majority of other denizens were offspring of the apex of wealth and power. But was affluence the only thing they wanted to remove from our realm?

Time to stop saying *I had no idea* … That California was rife with the KKK in the 1920-30s, infiltrating police forces and town councils, posting signs that read "Caucasian-only" at city limits [i]; that the list of suspected Sundown Towns in California numbers well over 100, that one of those town councils agreed to (and did) burn down an ethnic part of their city when one case of leprosy was discovered [ii]; that in the 1950s the first African-American teacher in the Magnolia School District (Orange County), was forced to quit one year later because she could not obtain housing; that a corporation in the 1920s and 30s, bidding to attract residents to a new development in Palos Verdes—the town adjacent to Chadwick School's property—published a booklet entitled *The Palos Verdes Protective Restrictions*, which stated "no person not of the white race (except servants and students) shall use or occupy any part of the property." [iii]

> Racial segregation in schools is an institutional complex. … Segregated education depends upon and feeds upon segregated churches, segregated businesses, segregated recreational facilities, and segregated neighborhoods.
>
> Raymond W. Mack
> "School Desegregation: Case Studies of Conflict and Change," (1968)

The advent of "segregation academies" was a phenomenon of the 1960s, mostly in the South, following Title VI in 1964, and nothing I can locate uses that term for private schools in California. All I can do is zig-zag through some of their stories, both oral and written in unreliable first-person memoir.

Until 1930, Mexicans, the dominant Hispanic national origin group, had been classified as white. A "Mexican" race category was added in the 1930 census.[v]

This paring of historical quotes validates an urban legend that there was a time and location in 20th century California when persons of Italian decent (or immigrants from Italy) had to prove they were Italian and not Mexican. My grandparents, who'd immigrated to New York in the first decade of the 20th century, migrated west to California in 1936. The 1940 census shows that my grandfather already lived in the house he owned until his death on Vine Street in Anaheim. (*How* he was able to buy a house, only 4 years after losing his Brooklyn house and business in the depression, remains a mystery). Both the 1930 and 1940 census list the Mazzas as White.

Mazza	Crescenzo	head	R	60	R	M	W	38	M	27	no	yes	Italy	Italy
	Anna	wife				F	W	33	M	23	no	yes	Italy	Italy
	Ralph	son				M	W	10	S			yes	New York	Italy
	Fortunata	daughter				F	W	8	S			yes	New York	Italy
	Marie	daughter				F	W	6	S			yes	New York	Italy

The footnote-referenced list of Sundown Towns in California names Anaheim as *Possible*, and nearby towns Orange and Garden Grove as *Probable*, but Santa Ana rates as *Surely*. Sundown Towns existed largely in the 20s and 30s, yet during WWII, at a meeting of the air raid wardens in Culver City (California) while planning to canvass the city to encourage people to abide by blackout policy, the wardens were "instructed … that when they went door to door, they should also circulate documents in which homeowners promised not to sell or rent to African Americans."[vi] Racial restrictions had been sewn into deeds from the beginning of the century until the Supreme Court case that made such restrictions illegitimate

The air raid wardens were to get …the petitions signed 100 percent; for if even one person balked at the idea the work would be useless. Mr. Teague declared, "You might find some trouble. There may be one person who says 'I don't mind if a Negro lives next door to me, or if I rent to a Negro.' Try to win them over but don't argue too much. I know how you feel if someone did talk to you like that. Deep down in my heart I would like to tell them a thing or two, but there is no use arguing too much, just turn their names over to me and I will send someone else to talk to them. We'll find a way!"

"The Hidden History of Culver City Racism." John Kent

(Shelley v. Kraemer in 1948 made them *unenforceable*. Finally in 1968 they were deemed *illegal*). Back at the notorious Los Angeles Realty Board, almost immediately after the landmark 1948 decision that supposedly made racially restrictive property agreements impotent, someone was already drafting a constitutional amendment to guarantee property owners the right to establish and maintain racial barriers in covenants. [vii]

San Pedro, California, is not listed as a Sundown Town of any level of possibility. The Mazza family first lived there upon arrival in California. The location of the Port of Los Angeles, San Pedro was heavily populated with dockworkers whose union hall had been attacked by klan members in 1927.[viii] My aunt's nickname, when she moved from San Pedro High School to Anaheim High for her 1938 senior year, was "Pedro." My father also attended San Pedro H.S. for a while—at his mother's insistence. The eldest child, Dad was two years behind his sister because he'd left school in 1934 when he was 14 to begin contributing to the family income. After the 1936 move from Brooklyn to California, Dad's father had wanted him to continue working to help support the family; the younger kids could get an education. The compromise between his parents was Dad's part-time job as a janitor for a start-up private school in San Pedro.

"Chadwick Open-air School was established on September 16, 1935, in the comfortable little home my husband had rented on Le Grande Terrace, San Pedro."[ix] Mrs. Chadwick's husband was a lt. commander in the U.S. Navy and assigned to the U.S.S. Nevada in Los Angeles Harbor. When the Commander's family joined him in

> Margaret Lee Chadwick, founder of Chadwick School, was always referred to as "Mrs. Chadwick" by both of my parents, so I'll keep the archaic honorific. In text boxes, in italic, I have quoted from her unpublished memoir.[ix]

San Pedro, from Colorado where their children attended a private day school, Mrs. Chadwick enrolled the children into public school. Soon her sons began returning home, minutes after starting out for school, complaining of being sick to their stomachs. "The repetition of this violent protest each day brought me to the school to find out what was wrong. Plenty! An impossible range of ages in each classroom, a mixture of languages and races, a distraught teacher obviously unable to cope with the situation, in fact a coughing, tubercular, nervous wreck." So, "When Chadwick Open-air School began in the playroom leading out to the garden, we were four pupils and one teacher." Mrs. Chadwick became an early pioneer in modern home schooling as an alternative to public schools (and for some familiar reasons).

The following year (1936-37), the original 4-pupil school was re-named *Chadwick Seaside School* and was housed in a rented residence in San Pedro, with two additional students (the children of two naval officers) added to the roll. (Chadwick points out that the house was owned by "an immigrant.") It might have been this school year, or more likely the next, that the son of an immigrant became the school's janitor.

In 2020 a hundred-year-old mansion on the Palos Verdes peninsula was put up for sale by its heirs. Probably the first such residence on the peninsula, it was built by Frank Vanderlip, a banker who'd also been assistant secretary of the treasury in the final years of the 19th century. He and a consortium of investors purchased the peninsula, and "later created a master plan to develop the entire area..." That "Master plan" must have included the aforementioned *Palos Verdes Protective Restrictions*.

Probably during the second year of Chadwick School in San Pedro, at a luncheon hosted by a woman who would become one of the foundation teachers two years later (this timing is left unexplained), Mrs. Chadwick was told (she gives no specific credit for the quote), "Mr. Vanderlip is eager to find the right person to establish a school on the Palos Verdes Peninsula." Mrs. Chadwick maneuvered to let Vanderlip know about her fledgling school in San Pedro, and then arranged to meet with him. How fast this took place, and when, is uncertain, but the name change from "open-air school" to "seaside school" in the second year is telltale.

After a rural farm upbringing in Illinois, Frank Vanderlip lived a Horatio Alger life in New York, eventually becoming an influential banker and assistant secretary of the treasury. His wife, notably, "worked tirelessly to champion women's rights, education, wartime relief projects and the New York Infirmary, where she presided over the board for many years. She chaired the New York State of Women Voters in the early 1900s and recruited Eleanor Roosevelt to serve on her board. Together they greatly influenced ending child labor, developing pensions for the elderly, full citizenship for women and federal aid for education." Vanderlip rescued the purchase of the Palos Verdes peninsula when an investment group almost defaulted; he did not see the land until 1913 when the sale was final. The following year, after WWI unraveled the first plans to develop the peninsula, "preliminary drawings were submitted to the investment group for an exclusive planned community reminiscent of Mediterranean villages."[x] The Vanderlip mansion was designed in 1916 and built in the following years.

But the senior Vanderlip, referred to as "The Father of Palos Verdes," who bought the property and was involved with the (nefarious) plans for development, died in 1937. Thus Mr. Vanderlip's donation of the land, between 1936 and 1937, so that Chadwick School could move to Palos Verdes in January 1938, is mystifying. Or was it actually the enlightened Mrs. Vanderlip who completed the transaction? For whatever reason, Mrs. Chadwick's memoir does not fill in this information; she only details Mr. Vanderlip's initial vision of a school on his property.

> He wondered whether we knew of the Scarborough School in New York City. ... so he recounted some of his reasons for starting that school and of his desire to have a sister school on the wild, beautiful acres he had bought here on the Palos Verdes Peninsula. He also described his plan of development of these acres which was to bring a number of well-to-do, cultivated families who would scatter over the sagebrush hills beautiful Italian villas, each with a magnificent view of the Pacific Ocean. Certainly it would be important to have a school of high standing available to these distinguished residents.
>
> The Japanese farmers who had already been cultivating various portions of the hills and furnishing the nearby towns with fresh vegetables and flowers were to be given permission to continue their cultivation of the land they had bought or leased.

Japanese farmers given permission to farm their own land, narrated without a trace of irony, even given the Japanese internment camps had already taken place at the time of her writing. Was Mrs. Chadwick simply reporting what Vanderlip said? Did she ever become aware of the covenants with racial barriers in the property Vanderlip's project had sold, not to mention the project manager's virulently racist rants included in 1922 advertisements for the land trust?

IN the history of every great race there has been, under varying circumstances, a fore-gathering of the best of its brains and blood.

Starting in the Himalayan Mountains, breaking through their passes, surging over India, then across Europe and finally, ever Westward across the Atlantic and the North American continent through countless ages, the Aryan (Caucasian) race is now assembling its flower on the shores of the Pacific, facing the ever-eastward flow of the Mongolian races. The men and women who, in increasing thousands, are coming to Southern California, and more particularly to Greater Los Angeles, are those who, by a peculiar process of natural selection, embody the success, the brains, the initiative, and the best blood of the American people.

This is being constantly evidenced in every test. Eighty per cent of our high school graduates enter the universities. Our athletes repeatedly have swept aside the best brawn of the greatest universities of the East. The marvelous development of Greater Los Angeles, while based upon limitless natural resources and advantages, is due to the superior average of intelligence here, which is putting these resources and advantages to use. Every possible evidence is indicative that here, within another, or, at the farthest, two generations, the Caucasian race will flower in a burst of genius in the arts, music, letters, science, and constructive achievement.

E. G. LEWIS
General Manager, Palos Verdes Estate.

VANDERLIP PRAISES PALOS VERDES PROJECT

Frank A. Vanderlip has written to E. G. Lewis, stating that the financing of the Palos Verdes Estates is one of the most notable works in city building in Southern California. The message read as follows:

"I consider the financing of the Palos Verdes project along sound lines, with competent direction of expenditures, one of most notable works in city building in Southern California, possibly in the world. The building of a planned city on Palos Verdes estates should offer an ideal ocean suburb to Los Angeles, where growth has been one of the marvels of the west. The utilization of these vast estates for homes should yield large dividends in satisfaction and pleasure to great numbers of ptople. I congratulate those capable of conceiving and executing such a program."

Chadwick School pre-dates Title VI (1964) which determined no private school can discriminate on the basis of race or it would lose non-profit status. It seems, then, unlikely that back in 1937 or 38, the media would question Chadwick's plans for diversity. But Mrs. Chadwick claims the opening of the new school site incited op-ed questions (no amount of searching press archives in Los Angeles County verifies this).

As our surprising buildings rose on the barren hills and the local newspapers announced the opening of Chadwick Seaside School, many questions were asked regarding what kind of school this was to be: For Rich or Poor? Girls or Boys? Younger or older? Brilliant or retarded? Black, White, Yellow, Christian, Jewish, Buddist [sic]? Physically able or Handicapped? For "All" was our answer, qualified by "For all within our ability to cope with each individual." That was a daring (almost bravado) response to a conservative community which at that time had hoped for a select school for the elite of the Peninsula.

Perhaps, when she wrote in 1978, Mrs. Chadwick asked the hypothetical question so she could (finally?) make her defense, and likely a tacit acknowledgement that she *had* been aware of the exclusionary intent of Vanderlip's planned development. Still, she tap-danced a line in the middle to satisfy that same conservative community.

> *Actually our aims were not exactly like the message of the Statue of Liberty … welcoming the poor, the oppressed, downtrodden, etc; our message might be summed up as follows: 'Come all ye who are not afraid of labour' [sic].*

In Mrs. Chadwick's memoir, the school in Palos Verdes did represent "a wide diversity of races, religions, riches …" The photographs she includes in her book do not bear out the first of this claim. Religions and "riches" don't show up as well in photographs. At least one student was Catholic, and not rich.

> In Mrs. Chadwick's book, there is information on one young woman of Asian descent, Chizuko Kubota, who immigrated from Japan in 1948. She lived (and assisted) in the Chadwick home and dorms, graduated and went to college, but remained the Chadwicks' "daughter."

In February 1938, when Chadwick Seaside School opened in its new, and current, location on the Palos Verdes Peninsula, the janitor from the San Pedro site was invited to move to Palos Verdes as well. That spring semester of 1938, Dad would have been 17 and finishing his sophomore year.

> *While all students worked at Chadwick, there were a number of boys and girls who had extra jobs that earned their board, room, and tuition. These students often turned out to be on the honor roll.*

I wonder if Dad didn't remember—chose not to remember—that he attended Chadwick School and graduated in the first class on the barter system; that he had continued to do janitorial work for his board

> *Out of both necessity and good fortune we early established a barter system, exchanging the services of highly qualified and concerned parents for the boarding or day tuition of their children.*

> *… The eleven graduates, first-borns in their individual families and now the first graduating class to emerge from Chadwick, all suffered a little from self-importance. They were a fascinating, difficult, and varied group of young people. They all went on to college …*

and tuition? *His* story was that as Chadwick School sought accreditation, the founders worried they might not have enough graduates go to college (to prove the school worthy of accreditation) and thus offered him not only an education but also a ride to the University of California. But Dad's story isn't borne out by Mrs. Chadwick's written history.

Chadwick school did get accredited in spring of 1941, just a year after the first graduating class. However, the letter granting accreditation specifically points out that graduates *starting in 1941* had "the privileges that go with the status of accrediting." So Dad's high school education was not accredited.

Seeking accreditation, Mrs. Chadwick says, was "an arduous task," and she felt she "was fighting the battle of Jericho to gain recognition for students of Chadwick to enter the colleges of their choice." If the privileges of accreditation would begin for the class of 1941, then the struggle to help graduates be able to be acknowledged as qualified by colleges would have only involved the first class of 1940.

Thus we scattered over the New England coast and over excellent Mid-West smaller colleges a good many fine young people. We gave the same kind of personal attention to our students applying to western colleges and again had great success.

While the other 10 graduates may have attended private (and out-of-state) universities, Dad attended the University of California, which was free to residents. To partially

What Dad saw in sorority houses made him determine that his female children would live at home when they went to college.

validate Dad's version, when the board of Chadwick School sponsored Dad's enrollment—paying,

"The two governing boards reaffirm the long established principle that state colleges and the University of California shall be tuition free to all residents of the state."
A Master Plan For Higher Education in California, 1960.

essentially just for his dorm, although he also worked as a janitor in a sorority house—they either wanted *all* of their graduates in college for their accreditation application, or they needed one in a California *public* university.

Mrs. Chadwick didn't specify the date she began seeking accreditation. Likely she would have to at least begin gathering information on the process as early as 1937 when she knew she was building a school on donated property in Palos Verdes. Would accreditation have required her graduates to be qualified for the California university system? Were the other graduates simply not interested in a public university? Why did the "students applying to Western colleges" require a separate sentence? Was matriculation at a public university necessary (or helpful) in accreditation because those requirements couldn't (at least at that time) be bent and/or influenced by power and money as might be the case at private colleges [xi]? Is this actually the function she needed from Dad? And did she already know this or have this plan when she invited him to graduate in Chadwick's first class? Undoubtedly the memories of what he was told at the time, and was told when he was applying to college, and was told later when he returned to the "Chadwick family" as a teacher, and in all his years as an alumni of the first class, would be conflated and unreliable.

Perhaps there was another layer to the barter system: an agreement that Dad would come back to Chadwick to teach after completing his degree. He did do that, but not until after WWII and finishing his education at San Francisco State College in spring 1949. So he'd returned to teach the same years as the 1950 blackface faculty basketball team. Either call it the end of the first half, or the beginning of the second half of the 20th century.

> "California hosted more amateur blackface shows per capita than any other state in the post-Civil War period. The shows and parades were so central to civic and campus life that it is difficult to find a university yearbook from the first half of the 20th century without a blackface image."
>
> Rhae Lynn Barnes, *Washington Post*, Feb 8, 2019

Dr. Barnes determined that blackface declined in the 1930s, then (temporarily) ended following school desegregation rulings in the 1960s. Barnes credits African American women activists who were so "horrified to discover that the music, poems, literature and plays to which their children were exposed [in newly desegregated schools] were forms of amateur blackface minstrelsy, [t]hey ran a national media campaign and filed legal cases to ban blackface performance, dress-up, and texts from schools and government institutions." The attempt to ban blackface through the courts was not successful, but the activists' effort largely pushed the "mass-commercialized empire of amateur blackface minstrelsy" out of popular use (until its more recent resurgence).

81

Before 1964, before Black activists had an impact taking on blackface, the "mass commercialized amateur minstrelsy" was evident at Chadwick School. On the drama page of the 1948 Chadwick yearbook, two of the six photographs show blackface performances. One seems clearly an Al Jolson replication. The other …

THREE LITTLE MAIDS FROM HARLEM

I think these are boys, but their gender is inconsequential, except that men dressing as women for dramatic parodies is problematic in similar ways.

The other photo captions on this yearbook drama page seem as though written by someone who had no idea the actual title of the performance. Only this caption appeared particular enough to be a clue as to the name of the play. Yet searching the caption led to only *one* hit, the name of a 1930s play, *Mamba's Daughters*, written by DuBose Heyward (who also wrote the novel *Porgy* and adapted it into *Porgy and Bess*). The play was said to have "a unique perspective not only of Charleston's racial tensions, but also of the unique subculture shared by Charleston's elite whites and poorer blacks." Despite what would now be called appropriation, the novel wasn't *meant* as a burlesque swipe at Blacks, and the original production, notwithstanding the deplorable lyrics, was cast in African American performers.

Did the drama club at Chadwick really choose to perform *Mamba's Daughters*, a play meant for a Black cast? One that had closed on Broadway in 1939? Did they make the selection as an excuse, as a *vehicle*, for doing a blackface performance? Was the caption really a direct reference to the title of the enactment, and, if not, how would the caption writer know of these obscure lyrics?

And had my mother, or any of the members of the 1950 faculty basketball team, seen this 1948 enactment? Were there any common denominators? Possibly there was one.

In 1948, the San Pedro Sun-Pilot ran a brief announcement that Chadwick School had presented "A Drama for the Ages," directed by Margaret Lee Chadwick, who also stood on the top row, far right in the 1950 faculty basketball team photo. This is not proof that Mrs. Chadwick directed other drama productions or had anything to do with the blackface performance in the 1948 yearbook. Her memoir indicates that "A Drama For the Ages" (a Biblical play) ran every year, and the school also annually produced a Gilbert & Sullivan, although it's unclear when this latter tradition began. Yet this circle is closing. *Mamba's Daughters* was called the "swing Mikado" in the 1939 review (above). *The Mikado* (Gilbert & Sullivan) contains a song called "Three Little Maids From School." Chadwick School did a production of *The Mikado* in 1959 (was this their second such production of this particular operetta?). *The Mikado* is now controversial every time it is staged, regarded as "oriental fetishism," objectification and caricaturization of Japanese culture. In addition, habitually, *The Mikado* has been cast with Caucasians, now scathingly termed *yellowface*.

The Mikado

Continuing the Chadwick tradition of annual Gilbert and Sullivan operattas, the high school this year presented "The Mikado" in two successful performances on May 1 and 2. Under the guidance of Miss

In 1959, Mom and Dad moved their four children off the Chadwick School property and 100 miles south to San Diego. So many practical reasons to do this: the small size of faculty housing at Chadwick, the low faculty pay when faculty lived in campus. But my two older sisters had already started in Chadwick classrooms, with schoolmates such as Dino Martin and Yul's Brenner's son Rocky, and I would be in kindergarten there in another year. It was time to leave before we made more than just childish alliances.

In fairness, my narrative also suffers from the unreliability of authorial selection. Both my parents' memories and Mrs. Chadwick's memoir suggest there was something different about Chadwick School from the stock image of "private boarding school" (e.g. Exeter, Choate, Westover, et al).

> *Hollywood in its heyday embraced Chadwick, bringing in the children of many famous stars; doctors ... well-known architects and builders and engineers entrusted us ...; business executives brought their children ...; talented artists and musicians ...*

> *What was it that attracted all these parents? Was it our rural and beautiful location on the Palos Verdes Peninsula? Was it our reputation for being a country school trying to be self-sustaining where all students had to work for the general good as well as do their own chores?*

> *The farm was supplying for our tables fine hams, bacon, chicken, eggs, rabbits. In those far-off days it was our plan to have a self-sustaining country school with gardens, orchards, stables ...*

> *... each boarding student was given the responsibility of caring for his or her own quarters... ... all meals [served] family style with a faculty and a senior heading up six students of assorted ages; a hymn of thanks played before each meal; ... instill good table manners; involve all students on a rotating basis as waiters bringing food and clearing tables ...*

> *... students from many different countries ... living together inevitably led to a broader and deeper understanding of human nature, likenesses and differences. The rich young man from Iran found it necessary to discard a number of his customs and beliefs in order to date the American girl to whom he was greatly attracted. The brusque American scholar learned something of courtesy and good manners from a brilliant Japanese student ...*

In Mrs. Chadwick's listings of traditions and policies can be found much of the foundations for how our parents raised us. Among others, Liza Minelli, Christina Crawford (*Mommy Dearest*), Maureen Reagan, Joan Benny and George Burns' son Ronnie lived in this communal environment. While Mrs. Chadwick's definition of the benefits of diversity are outmoded, at least the concept of inter-racial dating isn't unthinkable.

But Mrs. Chadwick's account's selectivity glossed over the issue of discipline. She gives examples of what might earn a student a demerit, requiring extra work: leaving one's room dirty, cutting class, etc. She gives an example of what earned two students the use of the paddle she had made-to-order by the shop teacher: bullying, fighting. But she gives no stories of another type that were part of our parents' lore: children of the rich/famous who struggled with alcohol, drugs, and basic wild entitlement, plus the responses from parents (it was rage, and it was Edward G. Robinson) when such students were expelled.

Still, our parents determined it would be best for us if they left Chadwick. Dad would have been the only one of us to meet the departure with disappointment,

dispondency, or even despair, although so stoic it's possible no one noticed, certainly none of his four under-7-year-old children. If suddenly we were in suburbia instead of a rural seaside nirvana, it meant someone to the left had a pool, someone to the right had two basset hounds, someone across the street had a WWII parachute as a toy—we held the edges, threw it up and ran underneath, feeling we were each lost and alone in separate cavities of white silk. We weren't formed enough to mourn the rolling hills of native flora, the agarian fields and herds of sheep, the quiet dark nights, the maturing fruit trees and rabbit hutches and large vegetable patch our father had to leave behind and start over in a backyard itself no bigger than his former garden plot. We also were not the ones who had to adjust from a private

academy's high school chemestry and physics classes to rudimentary math in a suburban public junior high. I wonder how he didn't cry himself to sleep at night. I see I've closed another circle. At least I'm pretty sure he didn't return home in the morning, after only driving around the block, and throw up his breakfast.

Notes (including un-footnoted text boxes):

[i] https://www.latimes.com/archives/la-xpm-1999-may-30-me-42577-story.html

[ii] https://sundown.tougaloo.edu/sundowntownsshow.php?state=CA

[iii] https://sundown.tougaloo.edu/sundowntownsshow.php?id=1093

[iv] John Kent, "The Hidden History of Culver City Racism." https://la.streetsblog.org/2019/04/05/the-hidden-history-of-culver-city-racism/#_edn15

[v] Instructions to 1930 Census Takers on Counting People by Race https://www.pewsocialtrends.org

[vi] John Kent, "The Hidden History of Culver City Racism." https://la.streetsblog.org/2019/04/05/the-hidden-history-of-culver-city-racism/#_edn15

[vii] IBID

[viii] https://www.latimes.com/archives/la-xpm-1999-may-30-me-42577-story.html

[ix] *A Dipperful of Humanity*, by Margaret Chadwick. San Pedro: Anchor Press. 1978. Future quotations from this book will be sans serif in boxed text

[x] https://southbay.goldenstate.is/the-vanderlips-at-100/

[xi] "[B]oth the University of California and California State University systems, require a diploma from an accredited high school," https://www.educationnext.org/k-12-accreditations-next-move-storied-guarantee-looks-to-accountability-2-0/

What Would Gin Say?

Danny Was Silent, but Gin Left Clues

Since my sister found the photo of our mother participating in a blackface basketball team, I've traveled numerous narrative corkscrew spirals, forward and back, crisscrossing my own line(s) of (faulty?) logic, following (and inventing) leads left in yearbooks, newspapers, and lore, seeking to understand her place (and therefore my place?) in whatever storm had that photo at its eye.

There's one more launch pad in the blackface photo. The young woman who wore no shoe polish, no charcoal, no stage makeup, none of whatever the 6 others had used on their faces.

Her name, written on the back of the photo, was Danny.

In 1971, twenty years married and raising five kids, our parents took us on a six-week cross-country tour in an over-the-cab camper pulling a pop-up tent-trailer. In addition to rendezvous with relatives spread from South Carolina to Maine, the trip also included Washington DC, Williamsburg, Jamestown, Niagara Falls, Yellowstone, and various other sites.

One of the shortest visits was on Cape Cod. On the way to see Oyster Pond where prehistoric horseshoe crabs come ashore and where our mother had learned to swim, we stopped at an (appropriately) Cape Cod cottage in Sandwich to call on two old ladies. They were Gin and Danny. Gin's last name was Chadwick, the same as the private school that had given our father a free education in the late 1930s. That's all we were told.

THE MAIN SHEET

MARCH, 1951   CHADWICK SCHOOL   VOL. I NO. III

MAZZAS' WEDDING HAS SMALL CAST

Mr. and Mrs. Ralph Mazza are at home to their friends at 229 34th St., Manhattan Beach, following their wedding at the Church of the New Jerusalem, San Diego, the afternoon of Feb.4. The marriage was the second of Chadwick teachers since the school was founded, culminating a campus romance.

The ceremony was performed by the Rev. Robert Young, brother of the bride, who also gave the bride away. His wife was matron-of-honor. Vincent Mazza, brother of the bridegroom, was best man.

The bride wore a strapless, light blue, ballerina-length dress with white veil and carried a bouquet of red roses. Mrs. Palmela Mathers, Chadwick house mother, caught the bride's bouquet at the reception held at the Young's San Diego home. Among 30 witnesses and reception guests were

SQUEAKY GETS MAN
* * * * * *
PAM SNAGS BOUQUET

(Cont. from Pg. 1) the following from Chadwick: Mrs. Chadwick, Mrs. Frances Champion, Mrs. Margaret Childs, Mrs. Matners, Mr. and Mrs. Dodd Young, and Mr. Jewett Dunham.

The newlyweds honeymooned at Laguna Beach Carmel, and San Francisco.

Mrs. Mazza, physical education instructor at Chadwick, is a graduate of Sergent college. Mr.Mazza, a 1940 graduate of Chadwick and a science teacher here, took his BA degree at San Francisco State College following earlier work at the University of California, Berkeley. He is a World War II vet, holds a captain's commission in the Army Reserve Corps, and is expecting a call to active duty.

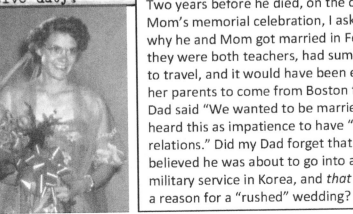

Why did Mom have this nickname? We don't know, only that she shed it after Squeaky Fromme attempted to shoot President Ford.

First column:
This student newspaper was nice enough to give their address to the entire student body.
Mom & Dad's wedding was the second to "culminate" a Chadwick School faculty romance. The 1947-51 yearbooks don't assist in naming the first such culmination. I'd like to offer that it was Gin and Danny, although without an avenue toward "legal" marriage, for sure this student reporter meant another couple.
The Swedenborgian Church of North America in San Diego will be the location of this narrative's final scene.
Second column:
Dad was in the first graduating class in 1940 because he'd been the school's janitor close to when it was founded, not because his family was one of the peninsula's "elite."

Why did Mom not wear traditional white? We never asked. We never assumed it had anything to do with virginity. We all embraced the apparent rejection of tradition, and she never proposed or even suggested white wedding dresses (or, in my case, even a wedding).

Two years before he died, on the day of Mom's memorial celebration, I asked Dad why he and Mom got married in February — they were both teachers, had summers free to travel, and it would have been easier for her parents to come from Boston to attend. Dad said "We wanted to be married." I heard this as impatience to have "marital relations." Did my Dad forget that he believed he was about to go into active military service in Korea, and *that* might be a reason for a "rushed" wedding?

For a boarding school launched in 1935 that began hiring teachers in 1937—one that also boarded single faculty—only two faculty romances leading to marriage by 1951 is a low frequency. I'll maintain our parents would have been *third*, if the counting included Gin and Danny.

> What causes a personal essayist to write about events long before memory, sometimes decades before birth? To continually return to a school I never attended, add a religion I never engaged in, many people I never knew. As I dig through earlier times, previous eras, people long dead, what do I hope this will add to my life, my identity, my perception of myself? I know there's an answer, just not quite what it is.

In her memoir about founding and expanding Chadwick School, Margaret Chadwick wrote, "Early on campus were the Chadwick sisters, my husband's nieces ... Both were somewhat bewildered by the complexity of their assignments which ranged from academic classes, to physical education, music to hard manual labor. *Barbara* escaped rather early by marrying a promising young lawyer... *Virginia* [Gin] stayed on for over thirty years…"

Dad told us, when he became a more gregarious old man, that Mrs. Chadwick had wanted him to be romantically involved with her niece, Gin, who had come to California from Massachusetts to teach in 1938. That was the year after the school moved from existing in a house in San Pedro to its own campus on the Palos Verdes Peninsula. Gin was a 23-year-old multi-subject junior-high teacher when Dad was a 19-year-old senior. It's doubtful Mrs. Chadwick was suggesting a student-teacher affair, so is more probable that her prompting Dad to date Gin came in 1949 when Dad returned to Chadwick School as a science teacher following WWII. At that time he was a 29-year-old "eligible" vet and Gin a 33-year-old never-married woman. According to census statistics, the era was a time of swiftly declining numbers of unmarried women, so "spinsters" [a word still used, studied, and railed against today] were to be pitied (or gossiped about?). Dad said, of Mrs. Chadwick's suggestion, he "wasn't interested."

What would Gin have said?

By 1949, another Virginia—Virginia Daniels—had been teaching at Chadwick for six years. "Danny" was older than Dad by those same six years. But her marital status fluctuated. Although she was hired as Virginia Daniels, and referred to as Miss Daniels in yearbooks, she was married in 1942, the year before starting at Chadwick. Mere months after her marriage date, her husband shipped to England, so doubtless a(nother) hasty military marriage.

By 1949, when Dad returned and was encouraged to date Gin, Danny was surely divorced (see sidebar).

Many of the testimonials from former students in Mrs. Chadwick's memoir, mention "Gin and Danny." But none of these is from a graduate before the early 50s. Still, several of these might have been students for 10 years.

In 1978 Mrs. Chadwick came this close to acknowledging their relationship : "'*Gin and Danny*' were pioneers who became 'Old Timers.' … They left Chadwick for New England in 1970, leaving a great vacancy on our Hill. On the Chadwick campus the names 'Gin and Danny' became linked as a most unusual pair of two highly individualistic personalities. Each one was esteemed for her particular gifts, and both were respected, admired, and loved. They shared a cottage on and off campus, and now on Cape Cod. Wherever they go, they create beauty, order, peace. They are truly a remarkable pair."

After finding no archive of California divorce records before 1961, I traced Danny's marital status by tracing the re-marriage of her husband. Through her marriage document and evidence of changing her last name on her social security record in 1942, I had the name of her husband, Donald Petrie. More marriage records gave me the date of his re-marriage in 1947. I still wanted to know when Danny was divorced, because it might (but admittedly might not) make a difference in when her relationship with Gin began. A 1944 newspaper item listing the whereabouts in Europe of local soldiers, said Donald Petrie's wife (giving no name) lived in Palos Verdes. Another such news item in 1945 said his wife (again no name) lived in Lomita, which is just east of Palos Verdes. Mom, a single female teacher at Chadwick starting in 1946, lived in a faculty dorm. According to Mom's photo records, new cottages for faculty were added in 1947, so it's possible in 1944 Danny lived in a dorm and in 1945 moved off campus to an apartment or rented house in Lomita—possibly because she moved in with Gin? However, after that, a 1947 party attendance list in the newspaper social pages lists a Virginia Chadwick of Rolling Hills, the actual city address of Chadwick School's buildings and faculty houses.

The students and faculty of Chadwick obviously saw Gin and Danny as a *pair*. Maybe they didn't (or wouldn't) use the word *couple*. Thirty years after Mrs. Chadwick's memoir, a blogger and part-time Chadwick archiver wrote a memory page for Gin after her 2008 death. In six paragraphs about Gin, this blogger did not mention Danny, did not even suggest Danny had existed. But she may have unintentionally alluded to Danny: "[Gin] described herself as a stern New Englander. [T]hat meant strict, proper, stoic... She ... was very private about her deepest secrets..."

Combine the 1940-50s era's laws and prejudices with Gin's "New Englander's" sense of propriety and privacy, and this kind of careful euphemism makes some sense. That the students and faculty revered Gin and Danny seems earnest. The 1948 yearbook was dedicated to Gin. Was there ever a parent who pulled a kid out of Gin's or Danny's class in homophobic intolerance? There's no way of knowing.

Very Best Wishes, Elinore, I hope you have a super time next year. Don't get snowed in!

Gin

DEDICATION

She cannot be called an easy teacher. In the eighth grade we worked hard for her, but when classes were over we played just as hard with her. That year gave us many happy memories. We still laugh about going to the circus, making taffy with Karo, and "tossing her a glass of milk."

Those of us who were not in her homeroom still find a generous and loyal friend in Miss Virginia, and we are all aware of the big contribution she has made to Chadwick School. In brief, she is a first-class person, friend, and teacher, but she herself is the first to admit that she is only a fourth-class skier! With affection, we dedicate this edition of the DOLPHIN to "Gin."

What would have been the difficulties in Gin and Danny's lives? Teaching at a private school, not going to LGBTQ bars or clubs, being committed to each other—all would have kept their daily work and private domesticity peaceful. Were they even aware they should be fearful?

In the 1930s, before Danny was in California, prohibition made all nightclubs illegal, so gay clubs were just as underground as straight ones. In an unincorporated part of L.A. County (now Sunset Strip), out of the jurisdiction of the L.A. police, the gay "culture was completely open and vibrant." [However] "The Pansy Craze ... came to a close once Prohibition ended and the Great Depression hit. And the 1940s and 1950s proved to be very hostile to the LGBTQ community."[i]

Until 1950, "cross dressing" (aka "gender inappropriate clothing") was illegal. "Being gay wasn't technically against the law—unless you were a teacher, a government employee, or, ironically, a licensed hairdresser,"[ii]

In 1947 at the beginning of McCarthyism's "red scare," there was a simultaneous "Lavender scare" which intended to purge the government of not only communists, but alcoholics (*habitual drunkenness*), gays and lesbians (*sexual perversion*), criminals and deadbeats (*financial irresponsibility*). All of these equated to *disloyalty.*[iii]

In 1953 President Dwight D. Eisenhower signed an executive order banning the employment of homosexuals by the federal government.[iv]

In 1951-52 California extended its "ban on immoral conduct for teachers with a law requiring school districts to be notified when teachers were arrested for sex crimes ... [and] to decertify teachers convicted of sex crimes..."[v] While this sounds commendable, the language of the law was not just aimed at pedophiles; forms of same-sex intimacy were, by law, until 1975, sex crimes.

In 1978, California state legislator John Briggs sponsored a ballot proposal which would've prohibited openly gay and lesbian teachers from working in the state's public schools. A startling move, probably in reaction to the 1975 consenting-adults law that took the teeth out of the aforementioned "ban on immoral conduct for teachers." But the attempt failed.

By the 1970s Gin and Danny were living on Cape Cod. Even after thirty years teaching at Chadwick School, Gin taught 9 more years in a public junior high in Massachusetts, while Danny, after 27 years at Chadwick, worked as an editor at a textbook publisher.

Using a genealogy site and a newspaper archive subscription—my two chief sources of research about private deceased individuals—in the period 1970 - 1992, I found virtually nothing about Danny other than where she lived on Cape Cod, a $10 donation made to Santa's Helpers, her 1992 Social Security death notice which listed no household members, and the cemetery location of her grave, which gave no further information nor a photo. For Gin, I found her "official" 2008 obituary in several newspapers, which, like the blogger's, did not mention Danny. As though programmed to preserve the privacy Gin prized, information about her on the genealogical site is limited to a timeline of the deaths of the rest of her immediate family and the location of her grave, a family plot. But from there I found an ultimate embrace of their relationship, in what is inscribed on that Boston Chadwick Family monument:

Frank G. Chadwick, Sr.
Elizabeth M. Chadwick
Ruth E. Chadwick
A. Virginia Chadwick
Virginia R. Daniels

Danny died two years before Ruth—an unmarried sister who also lived on Cape Cod —and 17 years before Gin. I can assume space was left on the stone for Ruth's and Gin's names to come after their mother's and before Danny's, and Ruth would have known this. Three of Gin's other siblings died after 2000 (only unmarried children are in the family gravesite) and they also would have also been aware of and agreed to Danny's inclusion in the family plot and stone. Like the Chadwick School family, Danny was likely received by Gin's family as part of the "unusual pair," perhaps as lifetime roommates; perhaps it was more frank than that. Although it may have been only as forthright as Gin wanted it to be.

In Another Cape Cod, Plus a Mission Revival
Mom snapped green beans on the long front porch of the Cape Cod ranch our parents' bought in Southern California in 1963. Sometimes she read her mail there. That's where I remember her being when she told me about Danny's death. It seems somehow important that she be snapping beans as she spoke.

Danny died in February 1992, not a season, even in California, when Mom would be snapping beans. This conversation happened many months afterward. Perhaps there was a handwritten letter on the table beside the colander of beans.

Mom was slightly agitated. She didn't ordinarily share "adult thoughts" with me, although I was in my 30s. She was reflecting on her old friend Gin Chadwick, how Gin had nursed Danny through her years of affliction with cancer, including keeping Danny at home through the ghastly last weeks and days. I know there was a point to her thinking about it and needing to say it (even to me). I think, in Mom's soliloquy, there was something unfair about Gin's situation, and I wonder if it was that Gin was now living on half the income she had before, and of course Danny's social security and/or pensions reverted to no one. In lamenting on how Gin had never wavered in her care, I do think Mom said "just like if they were married." But maybe that's wishful memory.

Sometimes we remember things we want to remember. But this one is attached to other memories as verification: that is, in years to come, as Mom and Dad got older and (accordingly?) more conservative, every time either of them would express a sentiment intolerant of gay orientation, I would think, "But Gin and Danny were your lifelong good friends and you knew about them."

That is to say, as much as I can claim I know anything, I know she knew.

As is common in elderly Americans of their generation, Mom answered an urge to return to her religion: The Swedenborgian Church of North America. In addition to the tendrils of gauzy connective filament (sidebar), it's where this story goes next.

The Mission Revival church structure was one of San Diego's oldest functioning church buildings, built in 1905. San Diego's Swedenborgian Church had been holding services there, between the neighborhoods of Hillcrest and University Heights, since 1927. In the 1970s Hillcrest became a LGBTQ haven. Couples purchased the original craftsman and mission revival houses and begin to (re)build the rundown community. Until 1960 in Palos Verdes, we attended the Swedenborgian Church's Wayfarer Chapel on the cliffs above the Pacific Ocean. After we moved to San Diego's city limits, Mom began bringing us to the Hillcrest church. Dad, a catholic, stayed home. When we relocated to the county, the trip to church would be a half hour—45 minutes counting parking and walking—so our attendance at the Swedenborgian Church ended.

Around thirty years later, retired, Mom resumed attendance at her church. She knew few of the members, even though the congregation was largely senior citizens. After she suffered a stroke in 1999, Dad began attending church with her. They often brought large bouquets of roses from their garden to adorn the small sanctuary.

Frank Vanderlip had purchased most of the Palos Verdes Peninsula prior to 1913 when he first saw the land. Before he died in 1937, Vanderlip donated a large parcel for a private boarding academy on the peninsula, so that the privileged who bought into his vision of a community of Mediterranean estates would have an "elite" school for their children. In the 1920s, Elizabeth Schellenberg, a member of the Swedenborgian Church of North America, who already lived in Palos Verdes, dreamed of a chapel there where "wayfarers could stop and rest." By the 1920s, when Vanderlip's development project began to sell estate sites, newspaper advertisements contained racist bombasts by the project manager, espousing that this project was for and by the "greatest race who ever lived." The contracts for purchase mandated the signer be Caucasian. In around 1939, Vanderlip's wife, Narcissa, another member of the Swedenborgian Church, donated land on the Palos Verdes bluffs for Schellenberg's dreamed-of chapel. In 1946, Schellenberg's daughter married Robert Young, pastor of the Swedenborgian Church in San Diego. Also in 1946, Robert Young's sister, Elinore, was hired by the private school in Palos Verdes. Elinore, a member of the Boston Swedenborgian Church, having just finished college, traveled 3000 miles with her parents to her first job as a physical education instructor. There she met and married Ralph Mazza. The school embodied aspects of a commune, as students shared the work of sustaining pork, chicken, eggs and produce. In the 1940s architect Lloyd Wright Jr. "found himself in complete accord with the positive outlook of the [Swedenborgian] Church and its emphasis on harmony between God's natural world and the inner world of mind and spirit," (Wayfarer Chapel website.) The cornerstone for the chapel Wright designed was laid in 1949, and the structure, made entirely of glass with redwood beams, was dedicated in 1951. A span of fifteen years that saw virulent racism in Southern California real estate development; a private school with no racial restrictions where children of the wealthy cleaned, worked in the laundry, and helped with the farm animals; and a lesser-known religion whose members included Johnny Appleseed, Helen Keller, Robert Frost, and a politician advocate for African-American suffrage.

"Swedenborg emphasizes the responsibility of all people to develop their own beliefs and live their lives accordingly...

...Our souls are individual finite forms of love, our bodies serving as mirrors of that inner essence...

This, then, is the living reality of Swedenborg's teachings. In stressing freedom, diversity, and individualism, he issued a challenge to individuals, churches, and other organizations to be committed to the human growth processes and to express their personal commitment in ways as diverse as their numbers. Sensitivity to, and respect for, each individual's 'internal church,' or spirituality, is what Swedenborgianism is really all about."

https://swedenborg.org/beliefs/tenets-of-swedenborgianism/ Note: The Swedenborgian Church of North America is distinct from The General Church of the New Jerusalem which is larger, newer, and more conservative but also bases its tenants on Emanuel Swedenborg's writings.

Wayfarer's Chapel 1952

San Diego Swedenborgian Church, now a Buddhist temple.

The San Diego Swedenborgian Church congregation was shrinking, so they maintained information tables at local neighborhood street fairs to lure new members. The tenants of the denomination, begun by a Swedish scientist, its frank atmosphere of inclusiveness, aided by the appointment of a lesbian pastor, could be attractive in the surrounding progressive communities. Membership didn't swell, but there was the invigoration of some new blood.

When California's Prop 8, re-establishing a law against marriage equality, was contentiously voted in, but then received its final *un*constitutional judgement in 2010, it was a period when religious denominations were debating and determining whether or not they would allow or sanctify same-sex marriages presided over by their priests/pastors. So it was roughly between 2009 and 2012 when Dad's somewhat high and foggy voice was heard in the church foyer after Sunday service, declaring his hope that *this* church would not begin to perform same-sex marriages.

Mom still struggled with processing language, especially in crowds, so she may not have understood, and neither one immediately perceived the tumult that began to stew. But while understanding conversation in a gathering could be impenetrable, Mom could read, and she had acquired a rudimentary ability at a computer to at least use email. She might call Dad over to read an email addressed to both of them from one of us, or she might have him read and correct her re-learned use of language in her messages, but he (adamantly) would not use the computer on his own. So, when the church's congregation began talking about what had been heard in the vestibule, and did their talking on the membership listserv, and when their "talking" rapidly turned into a determination that the person who'd spoken should be asked to leave the church … Mom was a comprehending member of the audience.

I don't know if she told him what was going on, had him read parts of the listserv, or if he actually got a telephone call from the pastor. Mom used the excuse that she couldn't understand enough to enjoy the service, and they stopped attending.

I know this happened because Mom told me. I remember we were in her computer room, the room that had been a bedroom for me and my two sisters. I was in her computer chair and she was in the extra chair where a second person could view the computer. But I think both of us were pushed away from the screen and looking at the birdfeeder out the window. These details are important because they solidify my memory of learning what had happened at the church. I am not able to fill in how either of them felt, except by inference from how (and *that*) she told the story. Telling an involved narrative was hardly easy for her. This one mattered, but in conflicting ways: loss of her ability to understand a church service, loss of feeling comfortable continuing to attend anyway, loyalty to her husband … But I'm not sure if the issue itself caused consternation.

And, too typically for me, I didn't ask Dad about the debacle. Maybe he didn't care. Maybe he was relieved. But something kinks my glands in grief, makes me want to shield him from what might have been a stab of disgrace, of rejection, and of having it done in the cowardly public forum of an email listserv. He'd been so often a silent, stern, even scary father, and now, when he had become vivacious—with friends, or even a group of newer faces—he was met with public castigation for (perhaps age-related?) lack of inhibition. His position to reject marriage rights for others is indefensible. If he'd said it at home, at our dinner table where he sat at the head, would I, or any of us, have had the valor to remind him of his old friends Gin & Danny, one caring for the other to the end? Why should he get a pass just because he'd become a glib old man who had an enormous boomerang smile too big for his wizened 5-foot body?

Eventually it wasn't his own humiliation that would have mattered most to him, because there was a subsequent loss. When Mom's congestive heart failure put her into at-home hospice for over a year; when that same computer room reverted back into a bedroom, this time with a hospital bed with a 24-our caregiver, Dad had become the one attending his spouse's slow passing. And when Dad tried, repeatedly, to get a retired pastor from The Swedenborgian Church to come to her bedside, he was, in effect, rebuffed.

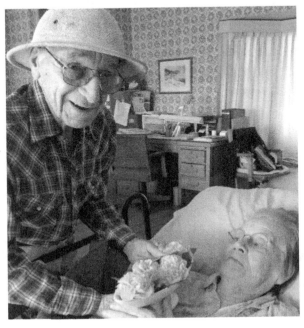

In 2015 when the Supreme Court ruled to enforce marriage rights beyond the man-woman delineation, Mom was no longer conscious or cognizant enough to know more than who was sitting at her bedside. Surely Dad noticed the opening of the United States to marriage equality, but this time he didn't say anything. And, again, I didn't ask—there'd be no point in that. But all of us, each in our own way, thanked him: For always kissing Mom goodnight and good morning, for bringing her flowers from his garden every day, for paying the $3000 a week for the 24-

hour care without flinching, for sitting beside the hospital bed holding her hand as he watched baseball even as she might sleep 50 minutes of every hour.

Receiving my thanks, he looked up from his recliner, his eyes hugely magnified behind his glasses, and said, "She's my mate."

What would Gin have said?

Notes:

[i] "The Pansy Craze: When gay nightlife in Los Angeles really kicked off," by Jenny Hamel, *Curious Coast*, May 11, 2018

[ii] "Before Stonewall, the Queer Revolution Started Right Here in Los Angeles," by Jason McGahan, Los Angeles Magazine, May 29, 2019

[iii] Johnson, David K. *The Lavender Scare*. Chicago, IL: The University of Chicago Press. (2004)

[iv] Executive Order #10450

[v] *LGBTQ America: A Theme Study of Lesbian, Gay, Bisexual, Transgender, and Queer History* Ed Megan E. Springate, National Park Foundation

We're Still Waiting

If, instead of my father, my mother had taken me to my routine physical exam at 11 years old, that it even happened at all would be missing from memory. Probably, in family scheduling, the only consideration was which parent was available after school for doctor appointments. It had always been Mom, but by 1967 she had gone back to college, plus there were two little boys at home. Whatever the logistics, nothing of the exam itself was memory-preserved. Certainly it was not invasive and I was draped with a cloth gown. I do know my father was in the exam room, because he answered the doctor's few questions. And I know that much because of the only clearly retained moment: the doctor asked, "menstruation?" and my father answered—with the boomerang-shaped smile he reserved for store clerks, non-immediate family, and, apparently, doctors—"we're still waiting."

We were? *He* was? I was dreading it.

Mom didn't think she and Dad would ever be in this position—a 3rd daughter about to menstruate. Just after they were married, during a faculty meeting at Chadwick school where they both boarded and taught, Mom wrote a letter to Dad (perhaps they were required to sit according to department; they obviously weren't beside each other).

I am bored stiff sitting here. I have been playing a little game naming our children.

Boy
1. Ralph Walter Mazza
2. David Robert "
3. Ralph Edward
4. Christopher Louis
5. Vincent Ralph

Girl
1. Patricia Ann
2. Ruth Elizabeth
3. Phyllis

We probably won't have as many girls —

Both of my older sisters' names appear in the "Girl" list, and my younger brothers' names are both present (first and middle, in various orders) in the "Boy" list. My name is not included. Were they caught unprepared? Possibly by her pre-set pronouncement that they would not "have as many girls."

103

Telling children idiosyncratic details about the day they were born might be a way mothers strive for a more thorough bond by folding time: an attempt to relive the emotion(s) the mother had in pregnancy and labor while also trying to share those experiences with the child who has no memory of being born. From something as mildly interesting as *Dad had to drive me all over the bumpy dirt roads to help labor progress, maybe that's why you get so carsick* ... to funny fathers' waiting room pranks that aren't very funny.

My younger brother's birth announcement was a narrative of a ruse pulled on Dad, already the father of three girls, to make him think his fourth child was also a girl, to make him publicly face *that* disappointment before allowing him the jubilation that he wasn't saddled with "another" girl.

Sure, daughters are fine ... but ... there's something *better*.

The prank may be a scene that never actually happened, or was enhanced for effect. One ultimate effect, however,

IT IS A BOY

"Girls are nice to have," said Dr. Warnock, and Mr. Mazza, who had been banking on a boy, after three girls, swallowed and gulped valiantly, "Sure, Doc, daughters are fine."

But it was a boy, and the Mazza chemistry and math classes led the cheers at the dinner announcement of the blessed event. And so it came to pass that Ralph Christopher, seven pounds and seven ounces, became on Jan. 23 last the first male bambino of Ralph and Elinore Mazza.

was that until I found it in my grandmother's photo album, I had believed this birth-proclamation lore was *my* birth announcement, and the joke was actually to make my father assume the doctor would say *Girls are nice ... but it's a boy!* and then pull the rug and see how disappointed he could be that it really *was* a girl. In reality the announcement of my birth was quite dull.

— BIRTHS —

Mrs. Dorothy Asher (former music teacher at Chadwick), daughter, November 17. — Ralph and Jean (MacCormick '48) Potter, daughter, January 17. — Charles and Marjorie (Hexter '43) Stein, daughter, January 24. — Ralph '40 and Elinore Mazza, their third daughter, January, 7.

In his telegram, Dad chose to pay for an extra word, yet maybe there was nothing behind the "another." His desire to add a boy to his family was, almost certainly, not a secret. It was something he'd wanted abstractly for over two years, and had hoped far more concretely during my mother's 3rd pregnancy. But, what did my father *really* feel in those first few moments around 2 a.m. in the father's waiting room after getting the news, in whatever way the news was actually conveyed? What *happened* in his physiology (heartrate, blood pressure, adrenalin release) and internal monologue when my gender was announced to him?

I have wondered this ever since hearing about the "girls are nice" stunt, and I have known about that tiny piece of family history as long as I can remember. So even if the prank never happened to him, it happened to me.

It was in my head again—his disappointment—in the broken months, which added up to equal a year, when I was scanning the 4000+ slides my mother took on the 35mm Leica my father brought home from Germany in 1946. After 1982 Mom switched to snapshots on her new Minolta; I was scanning many of those as well. But the slides, starting in 1950, were a more intoxicating, kaleidoscopic experience—I was trying to put them back into their original order after Mom had liberated them from projector magazines and attempted to divvy them up according to which child was featured. She had abandoned this project in the early 90s. When I took over care of her slides and began archiving, my inventory was her boxes of slides loosely organized by subject, three carousels she'd

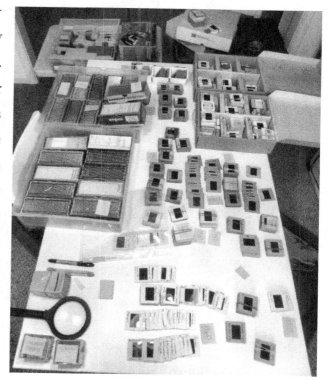

"successfully" distributed by child, plus over 20 still-full AireQuipt slide magazines. The aborted project showed me her possible reason for abandoning it: she would need at least two more carousels in addition to the two she'd finished for photos featuring her first child; she might need two or three carousels for photos featuring her second child; she was already finished with the single carousel for her 3rd child and needed no additional carousel. But she might need 5 to 8 carousels for the slides of her 4th and 5th children, the coveted boys.

I was using a slide scanner which required me to push each slide through, scan, eject by pushing in another, scan the next, etc. So, passing before my eyes and riveted brain: photo after photo after photo of my two older sisters, first as babies who can only lie on their backs, then on their stomachs, kicking feet and waving hands at the ends of dimpled arms. Then they are babies who can sit up on diapered butts, holding objects and inserting into mouths—colored toys as well as whole oranges, celery, cooking utensils or baby spoons, dolls, and cooked game-bird carcasses. They were plopped beside jack-o-lanterns and Christmas trees

(brought outside because indoor photography was still too difficult), naked in a sprinkler and placed *right beside* the board where Dad was crushing walnuts with a sledge hammer. As soon as they could stand on short wobbly legs, they were captured smelling flowers, pointing at anything, patting white bunnies on the lawn; posed beside Dad's limit of trout or ducks, his lemon tree laden with fruit, his German shepherd, his springer spaniel, the duck they named Ducky, showing off their Easter baskets and starched pinafores, their winter snowsuits, their rubber rain boots, their Davy Crockett hats, their Mouseketeer ears, gravely hanging their doll's clothing on a clothesline stretched 1-foot off the ground (a photo that tightens my throat with unnamable emotion).

This doesn't mean there are *no* pictures of me, but the numbers dwindle dramatically. With three children under six-years-old, even an insatiable photographer has to put the camera down more often. Mom herded us together into the same activity as often as possible, so photos exist of the three of us. It's enough to say that the number speaks for itself. Solo shots of me in my first year of life have a total under ten.

My sisters started school when I was 2-1/2, so my mother had a little time for photos of her remaining toddler. Then I began attending nursery school (at 3) and Mom went back to teaching physical education at Chadwick, where my father taught chemistry and where our family lived in a bungalow in sight of the gym and swimming pool across the agrarian fields of the 1950s Palos Verdes Peninsula.

This is a familiar grievance: Almost every third-or-later child in a family—a relatively stable family without violence, substance abuse or other aberrant disturbance, and middle-class enough to have commonly used cameras in the 50s, 60s and 70s—will at some point notice that there are significantly fewer baby pictures of the third than of the first and second children.

This observation will also frequently extend to baby keepsakes as well as the existence (or not) of a "babybook"—a practice that started around 1900 and reached its zenith in mid-century. In each family, the

> "'There are some wonderful accounts in those early baby books of babies having accidents and getting injured, which parents in the pre-war period find very amusing,' Golden says. 'I'm not convinced that babies stopped bumping their heads, or falling out of high chairs, but culturally you've learned that you don't record that—that becomes evidence of abuse.' Physical discipline was once so prominent that baby books had headings for 'My First Discipline.' In 1908, a mother wrote of her month-old infant: 'Baby received some discipline this morning. She refused to go to sleep before breakfast and also refused to be good.'" (Slate.com)

babybook's zenith would be the first baby. Each first baby's "first" carefully recorded, weekly then monthly heights and weights, first bath, first smile, first fingernail clippings saved; handwritten narratives about baby's first roll-over, first spit bubble, first finger-point, first solid food; and on up to the first birthday and cake-smeared face. In pre-war babybooks, pages

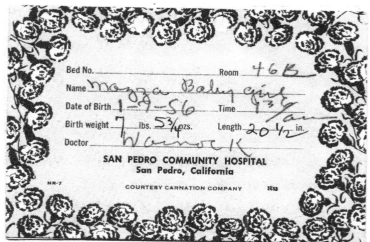

for first accident and first discipline were also included.

Among the remnants of my babybook—never in any kind of book, just a frayed box by the time it was given to me—are only one or two items from my first year.

Along with the disparity in the number of photos, baby book items speak a mother's obsession with a first child. But it also seems a birth month might have something to do with the occasion (or not) of children's birthday parties. For my mother's oldest child, on the occasion of her 2nd birthday in 1954, she wrote (*typed*) a narrative about a "celebration" involving a dozen neighborhood children invited for "supper" and party games. The original went into the baby book. I suspect she used carbon paper while typing to make copies to send to her mother and sister.

June 4, 1954

            (   ) is two years old! We celebrated this youthful event with a birthday party. The neighborhood friends and all the cousins made a total of twelve children for supper on June 4. The table was set in a party style that Mamma remembered having when she was a little girl — a party paper cloth with napkins, paper candy baskets which were filled with cracker jack and animal crackers, there were blow out favors, and in the center of the table was a big box all decorated with pink and green ribbons coming from beneath the cover and going to each place. The children came and we blew up all the baloons and tossed them all over the front room. When all the children were there we started playing the games. First we all set in a circle and played Button, Button, Who Has the Button? Then we went out in the back yard for a jelly bean hunt. Donnie won that game; he found 54 and Crystle was second with 33. (Lee found 2) After we all counted our jelly beans we joined hands in a big circle and played "Ring A Round the Rosies" We played that three times because   liked it so much. Then Donnie and Nicky joined hands to make the bridge for London Fridge. After a grand tug of war between the two sides we all went marching into the house singing Happy Birthday to   . We found our proper places at the beautiful table. We all pulled the little strings and prizes came popping out of the big box in the center. Next came plates of sandwiches and cups of punch for every one. After we were almost filled (we saved room for the surprise to come)   's birthday cake with two candles was placed right in front of   . Around the top and sides were frosted Toy Cookies set in pink frosting. Mmmm good. And there were ice cream cones too! Everyone was full, happy and tired as good byes were said.   's Birthday Party had been fun!

After that, photographs record my eldest sister's birthday parties in 1955, 56, 57, 58, 59, 60, and 1961. Her birthday was in June. For my January birthday, the first photo evidence that there was a party comes in 1964, my 8th. To be sure, indoor photography was not yet common or easy, and even in California too cold to move a party, or a baby outdoors. For my infant photos, she put my changing table under a window. I am an undefined silhouette, through the window the farm fields of Palos Verdes are green in winter sunshine.

The baby furniture in my parents' house was courtesy of the 1950s actor Sterling Hayden who had mysteriously left his children in my parents' care for a few weeks, then retrieved them and (according to my parents) left the country and abandoned all the furniture. My parents were asked to do this favor by Chadwick school's namesake and head-mistress. My parents were told, either by Hayden himself or Mrs. Chadwick, that his need to temporarily and secretly house his children was due his ongoing divorce proceedings. The Hayden children did not attend Chadwick—one was a baby and the other a toddler. There was some other way Mrs. Chadwick was acquainted with Hayden, or perhaps the go-between was one of any number of actors/actresses whose children attended the school, including Ronald Reagan. I reference Reagan because after Hollywood was first brought into the House Committee on Un-American Activities in the late 40s, Reagan testified in 1947 as president of the Screen Actors Guild (and did not name names, professing to believe that any political party had the right to exist, even if he disagreed with its policies); and Sterling Hayden testified there in 1951, confessing his own previous ties with the Communist Party and giving the committee other names. He later said in an interview, "the FBI made it very clear to me that, if I became an 'unfriendly witness,' I could damn well forget the custody of my children." Then in his autobiography said, "I don't think you have the foggiest notion of the contempt I have had for myself since the day I did that thing." My mother told me the hiding of Hayden's children and his subsequent fleeing the country would have happened around 1955, four years after his testimony, a period in which he made over a dozen films, seven in 1954-55 alone. Could my mother have been wrong and it was actually later than that? Hayden's child-custody was not resolved until 1958, and in 1959, according to *Time* Magazine, he defied a court order and sailed to Tahiti with his children. My parents moved from Chadwick School, taking Hayden's baby furniture with them, in 1959.

I don't think it was Dad's disappointment in my gender that caused my babyhood and toddler development to be considered less a miracle than those of my sisters. When the longed-for boy arrived three years later, the number of photographs of him didn't immediately match the first baby (but they do number more than five), and he also had a worn shoebox as a "baby

book." Later—when Little League and Cub Scouts started, when he and the 2nd boy who followed two years later started to hunt and fish and go on trips with our parents (after my sisters and I had stopped participating in family vacations due to marriages and/or jobs)—photos of my brothers mushroomed in number. When my mother did manage to make a whole 80-side carousel featuring me, at least 10 of those slides had to be taken from girl scout outings where I was one of eight or nine in the picture; and photographs of me with my father are not only infrequent but seem the perfunctory "here, hold the baby and I'll take everyone's picture."

And then there's my father's expression as he ogles his baby son.

Interesting to contemplate, decades afterwards, how artifacts support (or don't) my father's disappointment. But whether "all in my head" or in actuality somewhere north of that—either way, at the time and to this day, there has been impact. It may be faulty logic, *B follows A, therefore A caused B*: I was sure my father (or parents) were disappointed that I was not a boy, *therefore* I developed a distaste for my body and a phobic aspiration to never mature that went beyond tomboy-ism.

Also interesting to ponder *why* I remember certain clips of time. Like this one: In college, at my sister's rental house—in a neighborhood in San Diego where, in a few years, I

110

would have my own little rental house—my sister's post-navy pre-med husband came home from an interview for a lab assistant summer job which he did not get.

"*You* didn't get it? What were they looking for?" someone asked. (Me? Not sure.)

But I know his answer: "They wanted someone flat here," his hand hovering over the area of his crotch, "and bumpy here," the other hand hovering over his chest."

Did I hear an early version of white-male howling about hiring-quotas for women which displaced deserving men? If so, only in the background of a foregrounded private din: I was hearing him describe my Barbie™ dolls. And it was *Ken*™ I'd wanted my body to look like more than his girlfriend's. Or as TV's Ted Baxter put it: *God intended men and women to have intercourse, otherwise he'd have made people only one way, smooth all over.*

I had Barbie dolls because my next-older sister had them first. Our Barbie "games" involved setting up individual households then enacting story plots: problems they had to overcome, social maneuvering and consequences. My dolls were Midge™—blond Barbie's red-headed best friend—and Midge's likewise red-headed boyfriend, Allan™. (Mattel believed in homogeneity in relationships, and the subordination of red hair to blond. My sister and I both had dark brown hair.)

I was not, and not even close, a girl who wanted to look like Barbie. Around the time my sister drifted away from playing Barbie with me, I was experiencing daily agitation over realizing my "smooth all over" body was going to change, and my efforts to stop it from happening were not going to work. I knew my brothers had penises and I did not, but thus far—other than my brother using his to pee into the electric wall heater in order to hear it hiss (and talk about *stink*)—the physiological differences between us had only shown up in what the outside world said I wasn't allowed to do: wear jeans to school, have my own paper route, and play Little League were the three most immediate. In those conditions, who *wouldn't* rather be a boy.

And then there were the less political reasons I did not want to be female that didn't (at the time) bloom in my imagination as gendered, only in how distasteful *I* was ... both as-is and in-comparison-to.

An oft-told story in these narrative cogitations, but retold here with this added layer of invisible context: (despite a few photos to the contrary) I have zero memory of sitting in any way nestled with my father. Our mother read to us, and there were too many of us for everyone to be enfolded within her arms while she held the book. That I might have been the one in her lap for two years, my sisters on either side, I can't recall. Those are supposed to be such essential developmental years, why does life take them away from our memories? And why does life cause us to hang onto moments like this: My sisters now too old for a children's storybook, the audience was me and my two younger brothers. My mom only had two sides.

Here's how it works when your younger siblings are still cute and you're becoming gross: you help by wearing dirty socks and baggy underwear that shows.

My youngest brother would have been 2 or 3 and no longer on her lap while she read, so he was cuddled on one side, the other brother on her other side. The book had pictures. Sitting on the outer side of one of the brothers, against the back of my mother's arm, I tilted in to see. "Don't lean on me," she said, using her elbow to push me back. "You're too heavy."

It couldn't have been more than a year or two after being shoved away told I was too heavy —I was awakened, somehow, in our dark 3-bed dormitory-style bedroom, coming toward consciousness gradually enough that comprehension arrived before I moved: My two older sisters were talking about me.

I was, apparently, loathsome, gross, incomprehensibly repugnant.

My bed was the 3rd in a row of beds with heads up to the wall, mine the farthest from the door out to the hall and bathroom. A window seat bookcase ran along the far wall, then a gap about two feet wide, then my bed, another two-foot corridor and my sister's bed, a third corridor and my eldest sister's bed. The far strip of floor tended to collect my dirty clothes. They couldn't be seen unless one came to the foot of my bed and looked up the aisle. My sisters called it "the crack," or "Crissy's crack." It stunk, they said that night.

And: I breathed through my mouth, and I made a sound like "tehh" with each breath, and I stood with my back arched and belly sticking out, and I picked my toenails in bed (they could hear it), and I didn't wash my face in the morning so I always had sleep in my eyes. And—

"Are you sure she's asleep? Crissy? Crissy?"

A mortifying moment, but lasting more than a moment. I remember it over five decades later, how still I lay, listening.

It was 2nd, 3rd, maybe 4th grade. Before that, had I felt the distaste for my body, the revulsion that would morph and muddle the rest of my life?

> I had a female childhood name which was not "Crissy," but using it here, even in a context showing it's part of the past, is still too irksome to allow me to reveal. I eliminated that name in phases, finally completing the transformation to my unisex name over 20 years ago. I am not going to deadname myself here, a concept understood by transgenders, non-binaries, and those of us who have assumed this level of androgyny as well.

Psychologists say that our aversion to our own (and

> "One of the first blows to self-respect was learning that various emissions from the body are unacceptable … Psychoanalysts have long noted the unconscious mingling together in many men's minds of semen, urine, and feces. Toilet training taught the young boy what mother thought of the last two." [Same for females, except trade semen for menstrual blood.] "… Women's problems with shame at bleeding stem from a lifelong association with mother in which everything that emanates from the body is suspect."
>
> —Nancy Friday, *Men in Love*, 1980

all human) waste starts from our earliest perceptions of our mothers' (and fathers?) expressed displeasure in our producing it. At first this is an equal playing field in body-loathing. Most boys will at least partially recover, and the burgeoning love of their own bodies could have something to do with how obviously preferable it was to be male. But for now, I'm going somewhere else. Tracing my body-loathing back to the dawn-of-memory via feces.

Remember the children's book, Everyone Poops? *It is meant to teach kids that defecating is a natural, healthy part of digestion, and it does so by illustrating a wide variety of creatures—dogs, cats, snakes, whales, hippos, little boys—happily defecating. But you know who you won't see defecating in that book, happily or unhappily? Women.*
"Women Poop. Sometimes At Work. Get Over It."
By Jessica Bennett and Amanda McCall, NYT Sept. 17, 2019

I *hated* that children's book—which I first saw as an adult—did not want to look at the pictures, did *not* laugh along with my then-husband who had actually *purchased* it even though neither he or I had children, or ever would have children, to teach not to hate their bodies.

Girls aren't born with poo shame—it's something they're taught. In "Psychology in the Bathroom,"
the psychologist Nicholas Haslam writes that girls tend to be toilet trained earlier than boys, learning
at a young age to neatly keep their bodily functions contained (our words, not his).

Bennett and McCall

I could go deeper into this area, especially in seeing how boys tend to split away from this shame early on (evidence: reactions to flatulence or willingness to engage in scatological humor)—which could be an applicable aspect of my own gender-disorientation, that I do not share those male traits—but, again, my use of "poo shame" here has to do with it being a primal example of my body-loathing, evidenced by one of my earliest memories, one which was obviously not assisted by a parent repeating a babyhood story over and over until I believed I could actually recall it. So, I know I actually remember the following event, and, like the recollection of waking to hear my sisters talking about my grossness, the *why do I remember?* has only to do with shame.

A blip image: my 3-year-old body perched on a toilet at the public nursery school I attended nearby Chadwick School … and the way my bare butt might have fallen somewhat into the hole of the toilet seat because my thighs could not have made enough contact with the rim to hold me seated upright. Was anyone helping me? The memory doesn't say. That impression is followed by a connected one: the (abhorrent) sight of my yellowish diarrhea in the bowl. I must have looked behind me after my feet were back on the floor. The teacher must have had some kind of response. Or she may have told my mother (with some kind of abhorrence) in front me when I was picked up that day. And I must have already known how parents react when dreadful things come out of one's body, especially when they're not supposed to, or in some form that does not make them acceptable even if deposited in the correct receptacle.

" [Women] have been raised to believe that the area between our legs is untouchable, dirty. We have come to loathe the sight and smell of our genitals. It is an unnatural learned revulsion that has been deeply and dutifully taken as part of the early mother/child love exchange."
— Nancy Friday, *Women on Top*, 1991

[But men's association with mother's distaste for bodily emissions has a disconnect: realizing that mother has no penis.] "… if men bled once a month they'd probably have turned it into a triumphant assertion of manhood. Which is what they've done, instead, with semen."
— Nancy Friday, *Men in Love*, 1980

"Female genitals look like they previously had a penis, it was ripped out and now they have a gaping wound … that never healed."
— Shere Hite, *The Hite Report on Male Sexuality*, 1978

From that "normal" toilet-shame memory of a toddler, to a deviant dread of puberty—from age 3 to around 11 or 12 (or whenever Mom told be about "the bleeding")—there are seven or eight years that include (in addition to that desolate night hearing my grossness discussed):

- An early, daybreak-of-memory hero was Mary Martin. In 1960, '63 and '66, NBC broadcast a television stage version of the Broadway musical *Peter Pan*, starring Mary Martin as Peter Pan. I might not have realized Martin was not male; it might simply have been *Peter* who was my hero. But how appropriate for the "boy who refused to grow up" to lure my attention, considering the skewed Peter-Pan syndrome I would engage at pubescence.

> "…Broadway producer Charles Frohman [first] suggested that a woman should play the role [at the turn of the 20th century] because casting a boy would affect the rest of the children in the ensemble, who "would have to be scaled down in proportion." —Lynette Rice, *People*, 2014

- Our mother liked to dress my sisters and me in girl clothes. But we referred to girl fashion on the outer edges of feminine as "pewey" and girls who dressed that way were "pews." Pronounced like the bench in a church, but interestingly, a onomatopoeia referring to odor. Maybe they reeked of weakness, or something similarly ominous. My sisters seemed to have recovered from this bias in adolescence, but I did not.

"Pewey" preferred

- Fantasy games of vicarious *male* lives, Superman, Engineer Bill, cops-&-robbers, civil war (during the 1964-6 centennial which produced toys like the Remco Johnny Reb Cannon™ that actually "shot" out a hard plastic ball the size of a baseball) … apexed when I invented a solo fantasy game whereby I lived at a boys' boarding school. In my reverie, we at the school were orphans (had we somehow disappointed our parents?) but we each had a pony.

Engineer Bill

- Starting with Dick Van Dyke in *Mary Poppins*, through the Barkley boys in *The Big Valley*, David Birney in *Testimony of Two Men*, Robert Redford in *Electric Horseman*, Colin Firth in *Pride & Prejudice*, and recently, Johnny Flynn in *Emma*, I've always admired handsome, slim men in formal wear, in Victorian gentlemen's garb, or in Levis, but instead of wanting to be the lovely women invariably paired with these actors, I imagined the great pleasure it must give men to look like that.

- In Barbie games, which often included a 3rd person spoken narrative, Barbie & Midge didn't, but Allan and Ken *did* go pee: despite the absence of penises, we signaled their urination by the "sound" of their pee hitting the toilet water being like a bugle playing reveille—thus folding boys' love of and homage to their bodies into our play.

The next time-stroll starts with my mother's warning: *someday you'll find blood in your underwear.* I'm sure she didn't mean it as a distress signal; she wasn't blending dissemination of information with the spread of fear. But that was the result.

This knowledge about the looming and loathsome changes came in the 4th grade, at some point before the physical exam with my father present. By the time my father proclaimed "we're still waiting," I was already dreading. I've read and heard about girls and young women who yearn for their periods to start, to be given that signal of adulthood

> "I actually looked forward to my first period, longed for it, wanted it, *prayed* for it. … *please let me get my period today…* I used to chant this on the toilet seat, wiping myself again and again and hoping to find at least a tiny spot of blood."
> — Erica Jong, *Fear of Flying*

and the rights and pleasures therein. The *why* for my dread is so layered, all I can do is offer the preceding bullet-points, and perhaps some of the following that came just before being told about menstruation, during the trepidation, *and* after the arrival of blood:

- One night at dinner, my youngest brother, who would have been around 8 years old, told a story that involved his friend saying that "girls have a hairy puss." My eldest sister was 18. Our mother, seeing my sister's face flush, assumed she was the only one who was mortified. She chastised my brother on my sister's account. But, hearing his words, *seeing* my sister's mortification, validated my shame and terror.

- If that younger brother was 8, the other brother was 10, and they were in Little League. There were at least 2 afternoons a week spent by myself, barred from participating, wandering the Little League complex, dreaming of being discovered by a big league scout, while my brothers' games happened and my parents either watched, staffed the snack bar, kept score, or served other parental duties. (In 1974, how I hated girls who were allowed to have what was denied me when Little League stopped its gender exclusivity.)

- It felt like a glimmer of something similar to *hope* (but what would *this* make seem more possible?) or at least *optimism* (but what did it make more likely?) when my mother found an advertisement for the Presidential Physical Fitness Award in Life Magazine, featuring a 12-to-13-year-old boy who more than just resembled me.

"This proves that under my meek exterior I'm solid dynamite."

Every boy and girl who makes President Johnson's All America Team receives an award and this badge. Kids 10 to 17 are eligible. This is some kind of All America Team. Big guys have no advantage over little guys. Boys have no advantage over girls. This is a test of strength, speed and endurance. A test of all-around physical fitness. Tryouts will be held in schools all over the country. There's still time to get in shape. For information, write: President's Council on Physical Fitness Washington, D.C. 20203

I earned, instead, a lesser certificate:

- Perhaps the above was the impetus for this strange event: one night after my bath, I stood in the steam before dressing in pajamas, parted my hair on the side and combed it up and over, in a wet BrylCreem-looking style. I was so taken by the effect, I immediately went to the "den" where my parents watched TV and presented myself to them—still naked—saying, "Meet your new son!" I don't recall much about their reactions except probably my father's eyebrows rose above the frame of his glasses. No triangular smile.

- There was another nude incident before I put my body away. I've read that intimate body inspections using hand mirrors are not an exceptional phase in girls. I never did, and only infrequently appraised what was happening in the a full-length mirror in our communal bedroom. My main moments of privacy were on my bath-night. It was there I observed (with horror) the advent of body hair. I might've shaved it, but had no access to a razor. But I did find that with some pressure and twisting, I could get my emergent nipples to go flat again. One evening after my bath, after administering my anti-development therapy and returning to our room in my towel, but before putting on pajamas, I went naked to my sisters' desk where they were laughing about something in a book. Hands on hips, I was looking at what interested them, but one of them found something else interesting:

"Look what she's been doing!" She was staring, maybe even pointing, at the red irritation blooming on my remedied chest. I don't remember what was in the book on their desk.

- My opening (and closing) theatre experience was playing the male lead in a summer school production of "The Tall Stranger" (no relationship to the 1957 western film). I recall that none of the boys in the class wanted to try out, and the teacher was amused at having not only a girl, but the shortest girl in class be the tall stranger. Mary Martin admiration had come full circle. But this was the summer before 7th grade, and the two junior-high school years ahead brought the usual dress code demand of dresses and the barrage of taunts for my hairy legs, skirt length, ankle socks, no makeup, and hair that couldn't be washed every night in a bathroom I shared with 4 siblings. My time on the stage, and the gregariousness it required, were snuffed.

- With the help of my girl scout troop, but unbeknown to the leader (my mother), I passed myself off as a boy at camp. I was the leader's son. The camping event was called "troop camp," where individual troops from all over the county camped in separate sites at the large Girl Scout property, coming together for flag ceremonies or large campfires, but taking turns at the pool. While swimming, diving and bobbing in the pool, we conspired to keep my identity underwater should any girls from other troops pass by. Otherwise, my appearance alone worked, and worked well enough to earn me a crush from a girl in another troop. Being selected as "an object of desire" was something I had never experienced. This particular girl was not one of the cute or pretty ones. I felt magnanimity that I allowed her to think her interest was returned. We even exchanged addresses, and then, after camp during the new school year, exchanged letters. Disaster would have to be the outcome, especially when she announced  she planned to take a series of buses to get from her part of the county to mine, so I told her the truth. I don't recall if I explained any kind of reason for the ruse. One livid, outraged, insult-filled letter was my only punishment.

- That school year—which included mandated skirts/dresses and several incidents when I was pursued behind the curtains of the stage by two boys who pinned me and touched me through my clothes—I passed myself off as a boy again in order to have a paper route. It was a difficult-to-staff route because of the distance and hills it covered. I shared the route with another girl who'd obtained the assignment in her brother's name. When the route manager discovered who was delivering the papers, we were fired. 18 months later I shared another route in *my* younger brother's name; even the "delivery boy checking account" that banks allowed paperboys was in my brother's name. We both collected the money but *he* wrote the checks to pay for our papers, then he paid me half the profit.

- At some point before the paper routes, maybe before the girl-scout camp, but for sure *after* "The Tall Stranger," the waiting ended, menstruation began. It was the age of belts and fat pads. My 2nd older sister came home from a week spent working the Christmas rush at our uncle's bookstore in Orange County. After decorating our tree, the family sat in the living room. Maybe there was a fire, maybe chestnuts, maybe hot chocolate, some celebratory mood that came from the family ritual of trimming the tree. And my mom said to me, "Did you tell P— what happened this week?" This scene goes dark with my humiliation. But I am fairly certain (a) the cryptic question bypassed only my oblivious younger brothers, and (b) that my father was present.

What did I want or expect as an essential outcome of resistance to maturation? If I had known that self-starvation could prevent menstruation, would I have gone that route? Couldn't I have used paper route money to buy a razor and cause the emergence of pubic hair to seem delayed? Was my goal to escape my gender, or escape what my gender *meant*? From what I wasn't allowed to do, to the distressing things I was *expected* to do; from those disturbing and ugly genitals, to what I was expected to do *with* them … the conflicts did not make being female appealing. I'd developed a pronounced fear of sex itself, yet still thought it would be nice to have boys be interested in me—on *my* terms, which included *hold my hand, put your arm around me, want to protect me*—but no kissing, and needless to say no other *interaction with my flesh*. Where had this radical reaction come from? Certainly my father plays very little part, but does he have *no* role? Did I invent his role? Can anything that happened from this point forward help probe this numb lesion?

One partial answer came when I entered high school and the district abolished gendered dress codes. With relief, even relish, I chose androgyny. The androgyny I'd craved since avoiding "pewey" clothes, which had allowed me some of the aforementioned experiences, now allowed my school (i.e. public) appearance to provide me some satisfaction and occasional contentment, let me be safe from the criticism of female peers and the hands of male peers (but not-so-free from the criticism of male peers). Did I still have girl friends? Yes, and the two I had were very much on the girly side of the spectrum; they treated me with zero judgement. Did I want boys to like me? Yes, but expected them to do so without feminine conformity or shifting away from this:

What identity alternatives did I have?

A lesbian? I looked at that, briefly, and without fervor. I was not, never had been, and remain wholly uninterested in, even repelled by, female sexual anatomy. I didn't even touch myself.

I could (but couldn't really) become male.

The prevailing transgender process that existed in my teens and twenties amounted to hormone therapy *plus* elective (and/or cosmetic) surgery called "reassignment"—myth was they created a penis out of the tough vagina muscle (or visa versa). What a dull, numb penis I would have had. It was during college that I finally voiced my concern to my sister that I didn't have the slightest idea how people accomplished sex. She told me how to find my vagina with my middle finger while I was taking a bath. I was able to do that, but with zero sensation. I didn't understand what it meant to feel an urge to have that place penetrated.

Still there was no accepted out-in-society alternate option to surgery (that I was aware of) that could change gender identity merely by lifestyle (although I am now aware that people did do this then). And there was no recognized blur of *non-binary* in-between male and female. Even for someone who wanted to be "smooth all over."

Someone, also, who did crave attention from boys. A kind of attention I could have called "defending me" if I'd had the capacity to define what I wanted when I was 13 and 14. And in some fantasies it involved men or boys defending me *from* sex—rape-*rescue* fantasies, where the *rape* went no further than forced kissing.

What choices did anyone like me have? *Waiting* for a changed culture didn't seem one of them.

A recent study projected that just 48 percent of those 13 to 20 years old identify as exclusively heterosexual cisgender, (contrasted to 65 percent of millennials, who are at this writing 20 to 30 years old). Now my thoughts have to be phrased as questions, since I'm not qualified for anything else: Are the current era's gender-identity inflationary percentages due to a ballooning number of babies being born with the biologic / physiological causes of gender dysphoria— hermaphroditism, congenital adrenal hyperplasia, or androgen insensitivity syndrome? I know of a child whose mother is a smart, strong, energetic, successful woman with varied deep interests and

> "There is also growing evidence th[at] childhood abuse, neglect, maltreatment, and physical or sexual abuse may be associated with gender dysphoria. "
> -- Garima Garg; Raman Marwaha. Dysphoria (Sexual Identity Disorders) [Updated 2019 Dec 20]. In: *StatPearls*

passions, a forward-thinker who handles adversity with grace and proaction, who is usually optimistic even with substantial personal tribulations. This woman is deservedly adored by her child. The child is supported, encouraged, cherished by the mother. The child's father has all-but rejected his offspring, perpetrated the classic "nasty divorce" on his wife and children, and adopted a new family. That this 13-year-old has decided to be identified as non-binary—isn't it more likely a distressed cry to escape that "example" of maleness than a biological error?

From psychological need to be special and noticed, to psychological need to separate oneself from a body (or gender) that is repellant, with a cocktail of possible plot twists in-between: rejection by fathers, admiration for mothers (or vise versa), an extremity of preference given to a female sibling (or visa versa), an extremity of preference given by society to one gender, a noticeable preference given by parents to one gender, bullying (from anywhere, but possibly from parents), incest or mentor sexual abuse … a list of causes that could be unrelenting.

I didn't want to wear makeup, although I tried (on and off, starting at 18, ending for good in my 40s). I (still) didn't want to wear heels or skirts, although I tried (in my 30s). But actually having secondary male sex characteristics did not (all) make me happy. I liked having well-defined muscles without lifting weights. But I didn't want the mustache or beard that were developing (in my 30s). Likewise undesirable: hair on my chest or the thinning hair on my head (alopecia). The latter was my reason for seeking a medical opinion. Hormone-level tests did not turn up anything suspiciously off-kilter.

> For females in their mid-30s who have not had a pregnancy, hair loss could be a symptom of *androgenic alopecia* caused by early-onset changing levels of androgens. Androgen (the stem of the word *andr-* meaning *man* in Greek) is a steroid hormone that regulates the development and maintenance of male characteristics. Other male characteristics include muscle mass and body hair including chest hair and facial hair.

And during the decades I've been losing hair, plus living and working and partnering with men, at some point I accepted—without an articulated thought—that I didn't seek (or want) to act like, believe and respond like, sexually-desire like, or view myself in relation to the world … like a man. Apprehending all I've perceived about The American Male, that's not the identity that would make me whole. (The opportunities afforded males, certainly *yes*.) But I also didn't and don't want my identity to be based on, or start with "female" or (even less) "woman."

> "**wo**-" comes from the Old English "wifmon" and means "wife." "wifmon" means wife-man.

During the decades of my pre-puberty then coming-of-age, with his sons finally born and growing, there was really no reason for my father to feel disappointed about my gender.

Besides *we're still waiting*, his only outwardly displayed attitude in reference to my maturation was perhaps during monthly trips to FedCo when Mom would have to buy the large pink boxes of what Dad called "commodities." A word he also used when expressing exasperation that with "so many females in the house," the "necessary commodities" weren't properly maintained.

Still, between my ages of first-memory and 22, *disappointment* seemed the easiest sensation for my father to display. If not about my gender, what else was there? Did he show general disappointment to all of us? I'm sure they all have their stories to tell, just as I am aware there were plenty of other aspects of me that could deserve his disappointment. From my middle-kid outlook, I knew that he advocated for my eldest sister's high school schedule to include all the sciences and no typing or home-ec. He looked at my grades with a grunt (they were never wonderful). He joined my mother in showcasing my 2nd-oldest sister's musical talent at family gatherings. He never came to any of my school band concerts (I'm sure they were not wonderful). My sisters as well as one brother had good quality musical instruments purchased for them. When I played cello, I used a school instrument, then I bought my own trombone—the first non-male to play trombone at my school—for $20 (I'm confident my self-taught "practicing" did not sound wonderful).

For the record: The year my younger brother was old enough to get his first fishing pole and Garcia reel, I also found a pole and exact same reel under the Xmas tree.

True for every human: my father did not choose me. When my Mom was pregnant with me, if he'd been given a fairy-tale option to decide, he would have said "a son." They might have completed their family with three instead of five offspring—they didn't have to use *all* the names she'd listed. But neither my parents nor I would have wished for either of my brothers to not have been born.

It was, eventually, a man who did choose me, as I was, without make-up, with no skirts or heels, with more than my share of sexual dysfunction; too frequently irascible, in turns emphatic, autonomous, reclusive. For unknowable reasons, Mark chose me when we were 16. His choice never wavered even though it took 40 years of separate lives before beginning to be tested.

Mark was only able to know Dad (as more than the scary father of a teenaged girl) for a few years. One day they sat together on Dad's patio for a long while, talking. Mark, a foot taller than my father's 94-year-old shrunken five-feet, had harvested the top of Dad's tangerine tree, and they'd finished counting and adding

By the time he died, my Dad and I wore the same shirt size. I sleep in his undershirts and go to work in his cardigan.

to Dad's handwritten yearly tally. I didn't dare go join them for

During a holiday visit, a year after I scanned all those thousands of slides, we played them as a show on my brother's TV. Mark was sitting in a recliner, across the room from me. As the images of toddlers melted one to another, I could hear him murmuring "Oh," or "yes," and "there you are..." Embarrassed, I interrupted his reverie in *sotto-voce*, "That's not me," and "I'm not there." The slides are in chronological order. We hadn't even gotten to the year of my birth.

fear Mark was encountering my father's latter-years Fox-News opinions. But apparently what was going on was they were talking about me. No flashback (until *this* moment of writing) to the night I lay in the dark, paralyzed, listening to the dissection of my basic grossness. Mark later reported to me that my father was expressing fatherly pride. Mark may have maneuvered the subject to me (I'm sure he did), but he claims he didn't manipulate my Dad's communication of esteem. Not a viewpoint Dad ever said *to* me. Then again, how many opportunities did I give him?

After Mom died in the bedroom I'd shared with my sisters, Dad remained a little over a year in the house on the property they'd developed and nurtured for 50+ years—alone there for the first time. During that year, I visited once. We sat watching westerns and *Family Feud*, not talking much. He answered the phone every time it rang, gave long explanations to solicitors as to why he couldn't buy their product, almost got scammed a few times. But the call also could be his sister, his nephew, or one of his children. He said, "Every day I wonder who's going to call me today." Way too often it was my elder sisters or younger brothers, and not me.

The World Was Watching
(Were *We*?)

In 2008, while watching a documentary about 1968, my glands burned with a surge of visceral emotion during shaky video of smoke wafting and riot-armed police splitting the coursing throngs in Chicago who chanted *the whole world is watching.*

After *this*, I thought, how could the world not have progressed, been made better, when this generation came of age and came to power?

Naturally, in 2008, I would assume it was finally happening. Barack Obama was nominated in Denver forty years removed from Chicago 1968. Then he walked onto a stage in the same Chicago Grant Park that had seen the 1968 riots, to greet crowds celebrating his election as President.

But … the warless world, the hateless society, the healed environment … didn't happen.

Now—put *now* at summer 2020—as we search our pasts for the ways we may have helped it to not happen, there may be rocks to overturn in our parents' lives first. The worms exposed, in my case, are contradictions: during college Mom petitioned to allow her Black classmates to sleep in the same dorms as everyone else; then she participated in a blackface event 5 years later. It was 1950, before my half of the babyboom began, when many of those who marched in Selma might be from 5 to 15, when those being fire-hosed in Birmingham might be toddlers, when those being gassed in Chicago were being born …

In prior narrative ruminations since my sister found the photo of the blackface faculty basketball team, my exploration veered from the immediate particulars of our mother's life in the 40s, to the appalling deeply embedded systemic racism in early 20th century California real estate (an exposed tip of a volcano over what still boiled beneath). I knew my next venture into the same questions would have to start after my birth. I didn't realize, at the time of those previous forays, that the world would ask me to not delay. When I see the videos of brutality, sobbing, rage, crowds surging into streets, knowing *the whole world is watching* yet again—but this time with the indefensible backlash: barefaced heavily-armed combatants for white supremacy—I realize I have to seek a level of honesty I may not yet know how to locate. I only hope I can dig, and think, and sort, and maybe get somewhere while the world is still watching, even if it's not especially watching me.

Other than instructions for how to dress, table manners, and (possibly) how to hold the hose on a tree, most direct "instructive" communication from Mom that I can recall, toddler through kindergarten, was when she read aloud. Not that she didn't talk to us, but sometimes our direct questions were too silly to answer seriously, like when one of us asked what color our Dad's hair was, and she shot an answer into the back seat of the station wagon, "Blue."

The real thing
T-handle wrench

One of my older sisters clarified this for me by pointing out his hair was so dark blue that it looked black. Another time my sisters found something in a drawer and asked Mom what it was. "A thing," she replied. So from then on, although many objects could be called *things*, that one was the only object that was really a *thing*. We called it "the real thing." One sister could still describe it, the other sister realized what it must have been.

There's no way of knowing how our mother decided upon the books she read to us. Donated by other family members? Gleaned from the Salvation Army where our grandmother worked? Saved from her own childhood? Our books were threadbare and shabby; we and the books used each other into exhaustion.

Read-aloud was both poetry and stories: James Whitcomb Riley's "The Raggedy Man," Robert Lewis Stevenson's *A Child's Garden of Verses*, and Edward Lear's "The Owl and the Pussycat." In prose, there was Charles Kingsley's *The Water-Babies*; Rudyard Kipling's *Just-So Stories*; and *Babar the Elephant* by Jean De Brunhoff. The latter of these carries the

> Most of my life I called this character BarBar—adding the R in the name's first syllable because of hearing it, originally, from Mom's Boston accent.

most controversy, as the series of Babar books seems to justify colonialism. But we also listened to *Uncle Remus* stories. While Joel Chandler Harris might have collected and retold these stories to illustrate the arduous experiences in the "old South," his interpretation of Black dialect plus his estate's profit-making from appropriated material, not to mention the shameful caricature illustrations, has rendered them

> Voted Britain's favorite childhood poem as recently as 2014. We asked Mom what a runcible spoon was, and she may have given us an answer (Do I remember her saying it was a slotted spoon?), but even though "runcible spoon" is now defined as a spoon with fork tines at the end, at the time the poem was written, it was a nonsense word Lear invented that applied equally to a hat and a cat. Some have suggested "The Owl and the Pussycat" implied variances in gender in love couplings, but a little-known sequel poem does specify that the owl is male and the pussycat female. Is it about Victorian society and those who are different being forced to leave? Or is searching for deeper meaning an unnecessary distraction from the poem's appeal?

offensive. But simple book-collector research reveals the book Mom read from was a 1947

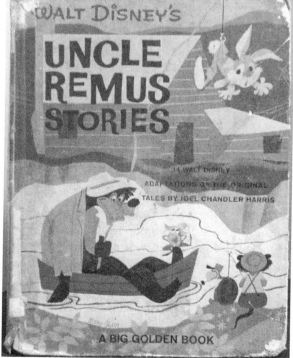

Mickey Mouse Club Book, *Walt Disney's Uncle Remus* or a 1964 Big Golden Book *Walt Disney's Uncle Remus*. While Mom read, I didn't see any illustrations other than the animals who were characterized (the fox, rabbit and bear). I didn't know what "Br'er" before their names meant. I don't know if any of us asked nor what the answer

> I've never seen *Song of the South*. Mom took us when theatres brought back Disney's animated *Sleeping Beauty* and *Cinderella*, in the 1960s. It's possible Harris's estate did not allow a re-release of *Song of the South*.

might have been.

A source of many of the stories and poems read aloud to us was *My Book House*, a set of books first published in 1920. It's possible our mother's parents had a set for their children and Mom, the youngest, brought the books west when she and Dad took a car trip to Boston and back with their first three children in 1958. Why this is important is that many sources say that "earlier versions" of *The Book House* contained one of the Uncle Remus stories plus the infamous *Little Black Sambo*, both of which were then replaced in a newer edition. (No source pinpoints the date this new edition appeared.) Since we were exposed to more than one Uncle Remus story, *The Book House* wasn't our introduction to that, but we still could have had the 1920 *Book House*, and that was our source for *The Story of Little Black Sambo*—this matters because one book collector reports that her 1920 edition of *The Book House* uses distinctly South Asian characters in the illustrations for *Sambo*. I am a poor backup resource: I have little memory of the illustrations for the character's colorful clothing, the tigers who threatened to eat him but were assuaged when he gave them his clothes, or the puddle of butter the tigers became when they fought over which one had the best wardrobe.

The Story of Little Black Sambo was first published in 1899 by a Scottish author who'd lived in India but never in the United States; in the end tigers chase each other around a tree and turn into butter then used by Sambo's mother to make pancakes.

Langston Hughes may have been the first to openly criticize the story as a "pickaninny storybook," not only because of the title and the name of the character, but because of the illustrations. Despite the story being clearly set in India, "it was the illustrations accompanying the narrative that garnered the attention of American civil rights activists in the 1930s and 1940s. In various editions of the book, Sambo is depicted as having very dark skin that is juxtaposed against the whites of his eyes and teeth, a broad nose, and a wide smile. ... Additionally, the term 'Sambo' had already gained currency in America as a black archetype, particularly, a black servant ..."[1] It's even possible that "Sambo"—whose origin as a racial slur dates to the early 20th century—became a slur *because* of the book, rather than being a known slur chosen for this character. Regardless, the book couldn't expect to keep that name and the offensive caricatured illustrations, so subsequently updated editions were released, starting in 1961, with newly named "Little Babaji" and South Asian characters.

When a 2003 edition was chosen for the Kirkus 2003 Editor's Choice list *despite* retaining the original title, Helen Bannerman's book was doomed to its current status as frankly racist.

[1] Jeyathurai, Dashini (4 April 2012). "The complicated racial politics of Little Black Sambo." *South Asian American Digital Archive (SAADA)*.

The more important layer to peel is how did any of these books affect the atmosphere or attitudes about different races in my earliest childhood home? My elementary class photos show a few Latino kids whose names were as routine as our own (a boy named Guy was considered to have an unusual name, whereas Pedro was just another name. I was bemused in junior high when Pedro suddenly became *Pete*, then in high school he was *Pedro* again.) But there are no African Americans in any school photos until junior high—and then just one in the whole school. I did hear the N-word on the playground, always white boys aiming it at each other. Did I know what it meant or understand the subtext of their insults? At some point I must have, but it wasn't a word I heard at home (exception below). There's a children's rhyme that starts "Eeny, meeny, miney, moe / catch a _____ by the toe." I learned it with a nonsense fill-in: *Minnow*. Catch a minnow by the toe. That minnows don't have toes didn't matter. Remember, there was also no such thing as a runcible spoon.

The only exception was when Dad used the word in reference to Brazil nuts. Any time he would have done this would have been in the company of some extended paternal family (grandparents, aunts, etc.) when conversation was boisterous, more unrestrained, sometimes a frenzy of talking-at-once. It must have loosened the adults' inhibitions. Easily we children could have learned the use of the word was considered okay. I can't explain why we didn't. I remember the first times my mouth tasted the utterance of *shit*, *bitch* and *fuck*. *That* was liberty. But not that other word.

"In the canonical Eeny Meeny, 'tiger' is standard in the second line, but this is a relatively recent revision."[1] Another South Asian context? "The shared genetics of all these counting-out ditties strongly imply an ür-Eeny Meeny. Several folklorists have proposed various etymologies based on the content of some versions." One theory is a Swahili poem brought to North America and/or British colonies with enslaved captives, and similarly, in 1982, a researcher proposed it derives from a Creole language spoken by displaced Africans. "The ... phrase *ine mina mana mu*, meaning 'my sister's children,' bears a very close phonological resemblance to 'Eeny, meeny, miny, mo.'" But could this could be a means to blame the 20th century replacement of *tiger* for *n---* on African Americans themselves.

[1]https://www.theparisreview.org/blog/2015/04/16/losing-count/

But the word returned in high school, in *Huckleberry Finn*, but it gets left behind in the debris of high school literature because I didn't finish the novel. I found *Huckleberry* as tedious as *The Scarlet Letter*. Eleventh grade English was problematic for a broader reason: every author we studied was male. Were they all white? Actually no, but conveniently neither the teacher

Interesting, considering I always assumed my aversion to the overuse of first-person POV in fiction was adult-onset, in 11th grade I didn't love *Huckleberry Finn* but was enthralled by *Knock on Any Door*. In fact, I'd preferred *Tom Sawyer* to Huckleberry, although it has the same problem with ghastly colloquialisms for characters of different races.

nor the book itself informed us that *Knock on Any Door* was written by an African American. Willard Motley's novel took place in exactly the (formerly) Italian-immigrant neighborhood where my university now sits. In the mid 90s a literary critic admitted "A couple of years ago I learned that the late Willard Motley was gay and Black and that he only rarely wrote about Blacks. …Motley said, in response to an obvious question [about this] … that he considered himself to be a member of the human race. There's no possibility of accepting that statement as anything but a pathetic dodge."[1] Consider that Motley would have given his answer before 1965, when he died. Taking into account he also used a pen-name when he wrote for *The Chicago Defender*, it's more likely he had other reasons for the "dodge." In his third novel I experienced a mixed-race relationship of throbbing tenderness.

The books may have all been written by men, but by including films in high school English, we absorbed a drama depicting jarring race issues by the first African American woman author to have a play performed on Broadway—Loraine Hansberry and the film adaption of *A Raisin in the Sun* (1959)—and one written by an Australian woman author depicting another form of mixed-race romance, *A Patch of Blue* (1965). Apparently, when this film was released in the South, scenes of Sidney Portier and Elizabeth Harman kissing were cut. I wish I could say for sure which version the school would have played for us in the 1970s. But I remember it being effectively poignant that the relationship had to succumb to its complexity.

I'd like to be able to examine how Motley's book and *A Patch of Blue* affected my romantic notions concerning the boys around me. But it could just as easily have been the "mixed race" relationship of Desi Arnaz and Lucille Ball, which I only learned later was considered mixed-race in the 1950s, despite Desi's "criolo" (European-descendants) privilege. When I was 9 years old, I determined that I would marry a man with dark hair parted and combed over who wore a suit with white shirt. Who looked like that? Desi … and Maxwell Smart. Naturally, that notion long gone—and junior high giving me no healthy concept of

---

[1] Lentricchia, Frank. "Last Will and Testament of an Ex-Literary Critic." Lingua Franca, 1996.

what a "boy liking me" meant—summer school before starting high school provided a titillating moment, its unique details unexamined by me at the time.

The summer Spanish class was likely a mix of 14- and 15-year-olds who didn't or barely knew each other, having come from any of three different junior highs. The gregarious and confident among us rose above the swarm, and Carlton was one of these. Smart, witty and not afraid to display it, and a little playfully roguish. He was also African American which, to me, went along with his personality— those lone Black guys in junior high had been popular on a level way above me. When one day Carlton turned the focus of his teasing onto me, it was extraordinary enough to have been flagged in my memory for fifty years. Carlton gave me a multiple-choice quiz. He

> A marked difference from junior high boys who'd teamed-up to pin me immobile so they could feel my body.

had written it out, but it was possibly copied out of a magazine. I was probably supposed to mark my answer and return it to him, and I likely did. But he also informed me (spoken aloud or written on the quiz? Maybe it was the title of the quiz?) it was meant to inform (who, him or me?) as to what kind of wife I would become:

The scene: you're washing dishes after dinner. Your husband comes up behind you, puts his arms around your waist and starts kissing your neck. Do you:
a) *Laugh and tell him wait til I finish here.*
b) *Push him away and tell him to help with the dishes.*
c) *Lean back into him and forget the dishes.*
d) *Ignore him and keep doing the dishes.*

My temptation might have been to answer with one that was not the obvious "right" choice. I don't remember if I did so. I have some kind of memory of Carlton and me standing somewhere in the room and the quiz being a topic of (mostly his) brief conversation. Maybe that was when I gave the finished quiz back to him. It's even possible there were additional multiple-choice questions and this is the one that was fused in memory. I even think I remember feeling a need to "correct" the impression I'd given Carlton about my potential as a dish-washing partner. I'd made a vow to

> Perhaps because in 10 years I would prove such an abject failure at what this question suggested about marital relations.

myself that I would let high school be a do-over, I would begin with all these new kids with a chance to escape my previous identity as a grubby nerd. This occasion would have been my first opportunity. Blowing it would have been a primary concern. That Carlton would give me his quiz was indeed a moment of immature sexual tension, perhaps my first without fear (except the fear of failing the quiz). That he was African American … was the implied thrill greater? Or was that due to his status as popular? Or was he popular because he stood out? And did he stand out because he was African American?

Nothing similar ever happened again between us.

The quiz was not memorable enough for Carlton to have even the slightest recollection. Turns out he'd developed an attraction for another girl in his other summer class—band. I was still a string player who played drums in band, so the summer band class was not open for me.

Carlton: Our parents never told either of us that we couldn't date. We were told that it wouldn't work out. Maureen's parents didn't know me nor my family, and the only knowledge they had of Blacks was what was being portrayed via the media of the day. Likewise I was the only Black in the band, and one of the 35 Blacks at an all white school of 2600+ students. Years later as an adult we both realized it wasn't racial prejudice that had our parents keeping us from the one another. It was our parents protecting two naive 14-year-olds from society. We could be friends, but dating was a no-no. I could attend an all white HS, because it was better than what they were forced to attend in HS. Mom sat me down and said, "your dad will not allow you bringing that girl to the house." The message was clear that I couldn't have a relationship with a Caucasian girl. Little did my mom know … It never died, just denied. Decades later, it was my father, an ordained minister....who married us.

I am a strong willed person. I paved a few roads being "the first" in a lot of things during my high school years. Self esteem was something I had a lot of. My dad gets credit for that. I wanted to join the navy and be a sailor, like him. He gave me a lecture that I was better than he was, and joining the service was out of the question.

Not only am I strong willed, but I am very independent. So I dated who I wanted to date. I just didn't bring them home. I didn't see it as being disobedient, I could think on my own. Just as my parents raised me.

There was and still is racial prejudice at our high school. I didn't allow it to stop my growth as a person. Our principal was proactive. He invited my mom and me to his house in El Cajon, (my dad was out to sea), to let my mom know that I would be safe at school.

The first boy I actively sought attention from was—before reading Motley or seeing *A Patch of Blue*—a trombone player in the band when I was a freshman and played tenor drum. The following year I'd taught myself trombone (the first non-male trombonist at the school) and experienced a range of what now would be sexual harassment, but perversely just told myself the boys "liked me." But I received none of that kind of "attention" from Adrian. He was tall and slim (face it, most boys were slim in the 70s), had long bushy hair, and was both intellectual and counter-culture. After my 9th grade birthday-party excursion to sled and throw snowballs in the local mountains—with 3 boys and 2 other girls—my Mom asked me which boy I liked. Thinking Adrian wonderful enough, I didn't mind telling her. Her response was disappointing, although I don't remember details of her expression or dialogue. I do know she told me he was "a different race" than me (which came as a surprise), and that "it wasn't fair to bring

Apparently it was a surprise to him as well. **"I have never personally identified as a POC, because that is not how I was brought up. I wasn't trying to "pass" or anything —just that I didn't have a culture that I identified with. I also didn't self-identify as a Jew. I knew that I was, from having a Jewish mother, but that is as far as it went. I never felt like a Chicano. That culture was completely foreign to me. I was just a regular, suburban, middle-class, kid of college-educated parents. I was aware that I was brown, just as I was aware I was Jewish, and that I had long hair. I have no memories of feeling discriminated against for any reason: brownness, Jewishness, or hairiness, though I knew it was a theoretical possibility. "**

And why wasn't he the one with whom I defied Mom's "suggestion/warning"? **"That was just my epic cluelessness. Plus I have never been romantically attracted to high intensity, which I perceived you as having then, and probably still now. You always seemed so fierce to me."**

mixed-race children into the world." There was no forbidding me to see him (no "seeing" was even going on), and any desire on my part to flout my mother's response was impeded by nothing ever developing between us. Obviously Adrian wasn't interested.

So it was easier to save being interested in a boy until one was interested in me. And when it happened, Mom had the same response because he was of Japanese heritage, in fact a "mixed race" child himself. She could have expressed other, more looming (and real) reasons to be wary of him—a very troubled boy whose career-navy father switched Japanese wives more than once; who then repeated his father's pattern as though girls-with-long-dark-hair were interchangeable parts; and who couldn't engage in physical contact without making it a

From here, "experiences with boys" was fraught with sexual aversion and dysfunction, which is not the subject here and inserts unnecessary complication, even though it directly impacts a pertinent college incident.

game of play-acted attack. Would I have heeded Mom if she could have given *this* warning?

Instead, repelled by the "mixed race children" argument, I continued dealing with this boy's problems and simply stopped telling Mom what happened in any involvements with males.

Hearing from these two men has strengthened my bewilderment over why our generation coming to middle age didn't make a bigger impact. But we are a small sampling, our "proactive" working- and middle-class county high school may not have been representative. When the demographics of the area changed in the 80s and 90s, the slinking-away of white families could be a lucid statement of a harsher reality.

So while I didn't regularly defy mom's implied or suggested standards—didn't sneak different clothes to school to change in the restroom, didn't smoke, wouldn't have known how to get drugs—her reaction to boys must have whetted an adolescent impulse of rebellion, either that or the inherent rush of the risqué mitigated the fact that for me there was little pleasure to be had in the whole ritual of "boyfriend." Not that I was solely interested in boys with an ethnic identity, but nor was there even such a long list of infatuations after high school that I can identify a pattern … except that they were usually "standouts" in some way, a college drum major, the band's trumpet soloist, a grad-student assistant to the directors, and a star football player.

There was an occasion when the college marching band traveled to perform at an away-game, and twenty band members would be allowed to fly on the team plane instead of the 10-hour bus trip that departed early Friday morning. The twenty band members were the band officers (I was administrative assistant) and those who had crucial Friday morning classes they couldn't miss. We boarded after the team was already settled in the best seats. So I ended up seated between two athletes, each of whom had over a foot-and-a-half of height on me and double my weight. Yet they were also *college men*, like the ones I knew, only more "important," and—even more provocative—they were Black. Before I became perilously dizzy with airsickness, I was given one player's phone number when he suggested I call him if I ever wanted to "get together."

Some two weeks later, I took the scrap of paper with the athlete's name and phone number from my wallet. I'd mulled over calling for several days. 1977 was prior to widespread use of phone answering machines. Very easily, he could have never been home any time I attempted to call. But I believe he answered the first time I gathered enough gumption to dial.

A decade or more ago, a literary journal asked me for a nonfiction piece, so I sent them a version of this story about the football player. They replied they were not going to publish it because "it wasn't special enough." I read their disappointment this way: nonfiction simply *must* be beyond the grind of life, it has to be the hyperbole of experience. The tacit 1970s nuances of a Black athlete arranging his dates with white girls so that he didn't call them and didn't go to their houses just wasn't "special" enough.

Few details about how the phone call went remain in my memory: A date was arranged, and I would meet him at his apartment, which turned out to be startlingly close to my parents' house, where I still lived.

Our date began with him wanting to dance, right there in his apartment. No need to panic about my inability to dance to upbeat music. His intent was to slow dance. I don't recall the music he played. Did he choose instrumental? R&B? Jazz? Rock? One would imagine that, whatever it was, any time I heard anything like it I'd remember him. Instead my trigger is a brand of cologne, and I do think of him every time I sense it.

But, I have to acknowledge, his being African American was part of the occasion. Afterwards around the holidays, my father reported to my uncle that I'd dated a football player, and when my uncle asked if I was going to see him again, my father's jovial exclamation was, "He's the wrong color!" Then, before I could think of it, my uncle corrected him, "Not the *wrong* color, a *different* color." I presume I would remember if Mom had anything to say; if she did, she didn't, this time, say it to me.

Because I'd stopped sharing personal quandaries with her, Mom would never know the real reason I wasn't going to see him again. The one date would be allowed to remain a sole demonstration of my grand rebellion. *My* progressiveness. *My* moral superiority. Because *it*, the date, had little to do with *him*. If the maturity or sophistication of either of the date's participants (particularly the one not him) had been higher, the occasion might not have played out only as my public moment of social revolution without consideration for his feelings, plans or wishes. More plainly: if I hadn't been an intrepid virgin, and if he hadn't intended for our rendezvous to begin, or at least end with sexual contact, then perhaps some coming-together of physical attraction and companionable sensibilities—whatever makes a "relationship" begin—would have occurred. Perhaps we could have accomplished something together, found a best friend and partner, supported each other through two widely diverse careers with wildly divergent pitfalls and tribulations. Or not. Basically he was a young athlete on the eve of becoming a professional, who was accustomed to girls who showed interest in him being … *interested*. I was an apprehensive virgin who knew in her fearful bones as soon as he suggested we slow dance in his living room that my bodily resistance to intimacy was not going to allow me to be seduced that evening. It had nothing to do with race.

The rest of the evening did have to do with race, was a show, was a selfish ego adventure. We went out to eat at a casual chicken-in-a-basket place, where the curious or startled looks we got from other customers was pleasantly exciting. We went to a dance club where the same looks were, again, pleasurably exhilarating. When he came to understand that there would be no sex this evening (I admitted my virginity to him, not wanting him to suppose I was rejecting him for the reasons my father would later believe), he benignly told me, as though he was ten years my senior instead of exactly my generation, that when I was ready, I could call him. We did kiss. He was drafted into the NFL the following April. I doubt he ever again thought about one humdrum evening in 1977 with a skittery girl from the marching band. That *she* remembered, that she included it in two books, as though some kind of admirable revolt, is actually almost revolting.

During my 20s, more preoccupied with myself and already habituated to not talking about my personal anguishes with my mother, I also wasn't spending a lot of time thinking about her social or political opinions. Being politically opposite from parents yet maintaining a family relationship wasn't *as* difficult in the 70s and 80s as it has since become. My first husband and I had a code word—something hackneyed like *Haley's Comet*—to change the subject or remove ourselves from the room if certain topics came up at family gatherings. Mom's school-teacher bridge-club had one Black member, a widow who brought her mother to parties. A house built on the hillside below my parents was bought by a Black couple, and my parents asked the husband, an ordained minister with his own church, to preside at my oldest sister's wedding. These snippets are as useless as "some of my best friends are Black." From Ronald Regan and his Welfare Queen and on into the O'Reilly spin machine, I was aware my parents had been on an escalator moving them farther and farther to the right. I'm not sure how Mom would have explained the young woman she'd once been who'd petitioned her college dean to allow two Black students to reside in the dorms with the rest of the female students, except the standard paradox that any POC she *knew* was "different" from the media-generalized whole.

But no incident displays the divide, hidden in plain sight, better than the 2008 election. I was due to visit my parents, but purposely put it off until the second half of November, even though Fox News, ubiquitous in their house in recent years, would be insufferable if also stomaching the "wrong" outcome. What made me think an Obama victory would mean subdued virulence? Perhaps I assumed I'd be buoyed by my joy, relief, optimism (now gone, replaced with unserviceable and ineffectual agitation). What I thought would *not* happen was for either parent to broach the subject with me. My father would remain blank-faced and eyes-magnified while his thick glasses reflected O'Rielly or Hannity. Mom, having been language-impaired by a stroke for 9 years, would keep it simple: showing me photographs and her latest watercolors.

Then … what were we talking about? We were in the room with her desk and her watercolors, my college bedroom. Our private conversations easily could turn to her frustrations with Dad's impatience over her aphasia-generated new grammar and vocabulary. She might quibble about things she wished my siblings would do instead of what they were doing. But, somehow, a worry about finances was in her dialogue, and her fear suddenly burst: "This new one, he's going to take all our money."

> "[W]hen McCain was talking about a pork-laden energy bill: "Who voted for it? You might never know—*that one*," McCain said, gesturing at Obama. "Who voted against it? Me." The phrase "that one" is being dissected by political observers, who, in a testament to the moment's weirdness, haven't come close to a consensus on its meaning. Was it an intentional sign of disrespect? Unintentional? A regrettable use of a common old-people term? Was it … *racist*?"
>
> "McCain Calls Obama 'That One': Why?" by Dan Amira, *New York Magazine*, October 2008

The second-half of the babyboom generation—too young for the 60s protests—tends to believe (without deliberating) that by 1970 we'd arrived at a more socially-advanced era, no more dress codes, the draft was gone we could vote at 18, girls no longer advised away from universities, HomeEc was for everyone, Title IX was passed. In 2006, when we were 50, a news article announced those born in the first year of the baby boom were turning 60. One of those listed was George W. Bush, still U.S. President. The article did not include Trump, born the same year.

I had to realize, at least by then, that for all the long-haired blue-jeaned activists of all races and genders, there were enough tie-and-blazer white boys born into a prep-school privilege that maintained their version of meritocracy … and who, as men, would still join the Elks. Here, I'll pass the baton back to Carlton.

> [Still,] We had classmates that let it me know that being Black was something they could exploit. They would harass me on band trips, because they could. There were no repercussions by the director. He didn't address discipline (race) issues until when we were sophomores and our band banquet was scheduled at the Elks Club. The Elks Club informed the school administration that the banquet couldn't be held there because the Elks refused admission to Blacks. The band could have the banquet there, but I wasn't welcome to attend. The band parents met with the director and my mom to discuss the issue. A parent spoke up at the meeting; stating I was a friend to his daughter. If I couldn't attend: neither would his daughters. He was Maureen's dad! Oh, the irony. I couldn't date his daughter, but I could attend a banquet with his daughters. The banquet was moved to a meeting room in the basement of Sears.

Of all the things I can remember and suss-out and research and inspect the unusual juxtapositions, this is the one I should have known.

DAILY TIMES-ADVOCATE, ESCONDIDO, CALIF. FRI. JULY 23, 1971

Elks retain white policy

NEW ORLEANS (AP) — For the third consecutive year, the Benevolent and Protective Order of Elks convention has voted down a move to let blacks join the fraternal organization.

E. Gene Fournace of Canton, Ohio, the new president—grand exalted ruler—of the Elks, said it is a question of constitutional rights.

The organization, he said, has the right under the First Amendment to admit whom it wants and to meet where it wishes in peaceful, private assembly.

The question came at the Thursday session when the 3,000 delegates were asked to delete the word "white" from the order's membership rules.

"This is part of our Elk constitution and had been in the statutes since 1880 or perhaps before," Fournace said. he Elks were founded in 1868 by a group of New York actors seeking mutual aid.

In separate resolutions, the convention voted to permit Fournace to suspend the racial requirement during his term and when any lodge is on federal property.

The first authority is apparently contingent on a Supreme Court ruling that private clubs may not exclude blacks. The second is designed to protect the group if the federal government moves to close private meetings of segregated clubs on federal property.

Fournace said that some non-white Hawaiians are members.

Fournace said the resolution to erase the racial qualification was offered by the Madison, Wis., lodge. There and in other cities and states, lodges have been threatened with revocation of their licenses to sell liquor on grounds of racial discrimination.

A two-thirds majority was needed for passage of the resolution to admit blacks and an estimated 40 per cent of the delegates voted for it. Voting was by a show of hands and no official count was taken, he said.

#MomToo

A gap in a resume supposedly tells a story, seldom a good one. Employers' imaginations fill in: got fired, didn't get tenure, living off unemployment. The resume is helpless to explain: raising children, caring for parents, disability or illness, recession.

Education		
1946	BS	Physical Education
1972		California Elementary Teaching Credential
Employment		
1946-51		Physical Education teacher K-12, Chadwick School
1951 – 73		housewife and mother
1973 - 1980		Elementary School teacher

Mom's work history seemed prototypical for the privileged young woman of her age, even if this facetious resume is not. Twenty-five years after her college degree, she finished requirements for her elementary teaching credential and went on the job market with a 20-year employment-history gap. At that same time, my 9th grade social science class was debating "should women work?" Evidently our little debate did not consider that 20 years of raising five children was *relentless* work.

I filled my looming resume gap with graduate school instead of children. Right before that invisible gap, I'd been preparing for a career in secondary education. I dropped the plan after a semester of practice teaching under the guidance a man 6 or 7 years older who spent as much time probing my anxiety about my virginity—perhaps even using it as a means to talk about his own marital sex disappointments—as he did "teach" me about teaching. Was my bewilderment, preoccupation, conflict, disinterest in and abandonment of teaching caused by the (average at best) teaching itself … or by his behavior? Behavior which, only two years later, would be called sexual harassment.

In 1980, the two forms of sexual harassment were identified: quid pro quo, and any (sexual) behavior that creates a hostile environment. There was other language to assist in defining "hostile": *intimidating, offensive, unreasonably interfering with the person's ability to work or learn,* and *unwelcome.*

But the *real* gap in Mom's resume was not the 20 years of being Mom. It also doesn't show up in the oral timeline we learned of her life. And both the brief gap, and what caused it, were thwarted before either derailed her. It's something she might have told me (but didn't) if I'd revealed to her what was going on during my student-teaching (but didn't).

She was 21-years-old in 1946. She'd graduated in June in Boston, then, with her parents, drove the 3,000 miles to California where her brother, through contacts he had among board members of a private school, had paved the way for her to begin teaching

physical education and boarding at Chadwick Seaside School in Palos Verdes. She had been a gregarious resident in college dorms. And in her 80s, Mom had not-so-secretly longed to move to assisted-living which she imagined as a boarding school for elders, where they slept in their dorm rooms, ate in a communal cafeteria, and met for games and activities in lounges. So boarding on her first job would not have been objectionable. Plus, she was single, female and very young; her brother lived 100 miles away—her parents were likely comforted by the school's faculty-boarding.

In 1946 Mom did not have a car. She went east for

summer vacations; she recalled a plane trip home where the plane seemed to stop in every state as it crossed the continent. Eventually (now a Californian) she had her own convertible. After one of her summer visits to Boston, she returned to Chadwick with her dog, so a car would have been necessary. In 1948 she took a photo of a male faculty member holding her dog. This young man, Ed Babbott, was new to Chadwick in 1948-49, so the photo would have been fall of 1948 … late fall, because that year Mom didn't return to work until

November. Included on the album page immediately following the young man and her dog, photos of a November 1948 fire that destroyed the music building.

Our mother told my sister that she resigned her job at Chadwick after the 1948 school year because there was a man who was flirting with her and he was the husband of a friend of hers. My sister points out that she's not sure Mom used the word *flirting*. What would Mom have said? *Bothering? Pestering?* And how would a parent tell a child a story like this, what kind of editing or screening or glossing-over might occur? Putting the event back together, with the kind of evidence available, admittedly is more speculation than fact, more fantasy than forensics. Maybe it's the only way I'll "hear" what she would have said if I'd learned (or hadn't *un*learned) to confide in her.

Using Mom's Chadwick yearbooks and a Chadwick promotional catalogue, I isolated married male faculty who were at Chadwick in both 1947-48 and 1948-49. I found two, Ray and Gilbert.

Gilbert Myers taught at Chadwick two years, the year before and year after Mom's 2-month gap. The catalogue gave his credentials as the U.S. Naval Academy and Harvard. A Faculty photo used *Captain* instead of *Mr.* The school's founder, Joe Chadwick, always went by *Commander*, as he was also retired USN. Captain Meyers lived in San Pedro, a navy town

Dad

where Commander Chadwick had lived when first stationed in California in the 1930s. The connection seems obvious for why and how Captain Myers was hired. The most interesting (for me) aspect of his Chadwick involvement is that he taught physics, which was Dad's field. Dad began teaching chemistry at Chadwick in Gilbert's final year, so they would have been close colleagues.

Gilbert's 1995 obituary in the *San Pedro News-Pilot* verified all the particulars, including his three years teaching at Chadwick. His wife was a women's-club "socialite" in San Pedro, hosting and organizing lectures, book clubs, and choral groups. Her age and public activities would have made her more than just an improbable "friend" of Mom's. Gilbert was 50 in 1948. While 50-year-old men have surely been known to flirt with 23-year-old women, it's doubtful. So, not him.

Ray Jahn's storyline is comparatively more provocative. He was only a year older than Mom. Since he was a freshman at Univ of Idaho in 1943, his year of graduation would be either 1946 or 1947, so he probably started at Chadwick the same year that Mom did.

Left to right, front row: Mr. Kales, Mrs. Gray, Mrs. Caluori, Mrs. Miller, Mrs. Hansen, Mrs. Buzolich, Miss Young, Mrs. Quinlin, Mrs. Chadwick, Mr. Chadwick, Mrs. Roessler, Mr. Burke, Miss Wernli, Mr. Hamner, Mrs. Norberg, Mr. Fatio, Mrs. Jahn, Mr. Jahn, and Mr. Gastren. Back row: Mr. Bovee, Miss Chadwick, Miss Collins, Mr. Buzolich, Miss Daniels, and Mr. Myers.

Mom was the K-12 girls physical education teacher. Her attire for her job, as shown in the faculty photo, was often the tunic she wore in college for team sports and activity classes. The tunic ends 10 to 12 inches above her knee while the prevailing fashion for the other women is just below the knee. Should this be a factor in how others "related to" her? No. *Was* it a factor? Was it a factor for me in 1989? My resume gap starting to close, I got a temporary

position as writer-in-residence at a college in another state. At the pre-semester dinner to introduce the new writer-in-residence and artist-in-residence, the latter sidled up to me during the mingling and said, "You get sexier every time I see you." Both of us married, but I couldn't claim the interest was unwelcome, nor that the tryst, lasting exactly the length of our residencies, was a man "bothering me," although there's no doubt I was distracted and couldn't function effectively in my job. Was I trying to look "sexy"? I can admit to going for *bohemian*. I was wearing ankle-high boots and a mid-length wraparound skirt I'd bought at a clothing bodega in Brooklyn eight years prior and wore only to job interviews (the last one in 1993) before switching back to androgyny. (Pants still an inauspicious choice for job interviews in the early 90s.) Hard to say if my attire provoked the artist's first approach, which I did not reject. And, going back to the beginning of my resume gap in 1979, that "master-teacher" mentoring my practice-teaching wrote in his observation log that I was "looking particularly lovely today," although at some point I was criticized by my university education supervisor for lack of professional attire (too many days in pants).

But while in 1946 Mom was a young woman who might easily have been noticed by a man near to her age, Ray Jahn had noticed something else. Mom and Dad's 1951 wedding announcement revealed they were the second Chadwick faculty

THE JAHNS

members to meet there and marry. Ray and Irma were first, their wedding date in Feb 1947 coming approximately six months

> **From the Chadwick School founder's memoir:**
>
> ...*Mrs. Irma Reddick*, ... [became our music teacher]. Irma was a warm, colorful and very talented musician, winning the hearts of all her students. She brought along her attractive daughter, Mary, thus joining the Barter Group. This lady was unforgettable – flashing brown eyes, smooth dark hair, a full, low-pitched voice, a robust love of life, and an unparalleled rapport with teen-agers. Among her many young admirers at Chadwick was our Librarian, a graduate of Pomona. Irma's vibrant spirit, her exceptional musical ability, and her way of relating to others proved irresistible to handsome Ray Jahn. In a simple ceremony, Irma and Ray were united in marriage in the living room of the Chadwick's home on campus. Irma and Ray had quite a long and a very happy marriage, interrupted not long ago by Irma's death [in 1972].

after Ray's first semester at Chadwick. The passage in the Chadwick memoir uses the adjectives *young* (for her admirers) and *handsome* (for Ray, one of those young admirers). This was the memoirist's genteel way of not saying that Irma was more than thirty years older than Ray.

In spring 1947, the Jahns placed a lost-and-found notice in the San Pedro newspaper for their missing toy dachshund and gave their address as Chadwick School (the dog in this photo from 1948 appears to be a terrier). Voter registration records for 1948 have the Jahns still at Chadwick School for their residence—this could have been in the spring before the California presidential primary. Mom resigned (temporarily) in June 1948. Neither of the Jahns are in the

1949-50 Chadwick faculty, and in September 1949 their home address is in San Pedro (from a newspaper wedding announcement for Mrs. Jahn's 21-year-old daughter). A ship manifest says they left for England in fall 1949 with the intention of staying for a year.

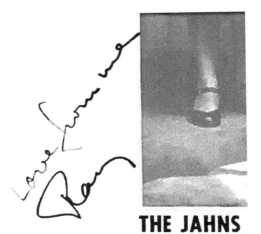

THE JAHNS

So, was it Ray Jahn? When Mom had her 1948 yearbook signed by friends and acquaintances, it's evident that the signers knew she'd given up her job and was returning home to Massachusetts. "Don't get snowed in," one said, "The kids are sick about your leaving," said another. Another bantered, "I shall miss seeing you next year with your boots and balloons." But Ray Jahn, signing beside his wife's foot, seemed more serious. Not *love from us*, but *from me*. Yes, the L-word is all-too easy to use in yearbooks, and I remember treasuring signatures from boys who dared to put "Love," before their names, meaning little by it. Nor would I have dared to use it as a yearbook signature. Nor did I use the less sincere popular-girl "Luv" or "Luff-ya." The artist-in-residence eventually used the L-word. He also used an F-word: *forever*.

Both had an expiration date, and I "sexually harassed" myself by understanding but still not believing.

But these weren't Mom's predicaments. Her oral account included that the bothering man's wife was a friend of hers. Like Mrs. Myers, 54-year-old Irma Jahn would have been at a phase of life where friendship with a 23-year-old would be improbable. And Mom, a voracious photo taker, has no pictures of any of the musical events that would have been Mrs. Jahn's arena. (Although, she did photograph extensive fire damage to the music building in 1948.)

Irma died in 1972 at 79 years old. Her last residence was in Missouri. Ray remarried in 1976 in California, then he returned to Missouri in 1979 until his death. His second wife was also older, but this time by only 2 years. She was 54 at the time of their marriage, nearly the same age as Irma when he'd married her in 1947. He had no children with either wife. Irma's

148

daughter was only three years younger than Mom. Despite the "Love from me," this stacking of facts tends to move Ray from the forefront as a person-of-interest for unwelcome flirting with Mom. It might be a safer (but still crass) assumption to wonder if Ray Jahn exhibited gerontophilia, or if he twice sought a *beard*.

My sister reminded me that while Mom's report included the man's wife being her friend, she had not specified that the man was Chadwick faculty. The Chadwick yearbooks' archaic use of *Miss*, *Mrs.* and *Mr.* instead of first names, makes it easy to locate the married women on the faculty. The chemistry teacher, Mrs. Gray, stands out, not only because she was on the faculty all of the significant years and then left after 1948-49, but because in her personal album Mom had a small professional portrait of Ingrid Gray, like a school photo made to give to friends and family. In 1946 Chadwick didn't do individual photos of either students or faculty, and the Mrs. Gray in the 1946-47 faculty photo was clearly not the same age as the Ingrid Gray school portrait in Mom's photo album. This more-than suggests that Mrs. Gray gave Mom the photo, a sign of some level of friendship.

In 1946 an Ingrid Carlson, born 1922, married a Robert D. Gray just as she was finishing her military service in the navy. This makes her three years older than Mom. Accounting for four years of college, then three years of naval duty, Ingrid was therefore on the same "track" as Mom to

begin her teaching career in 1946. Ingrid's husband continued with a career in the navy and they lived in nearby San Pedro.

As mentioned, Mom's 1948 yearbook contained signatures indicating her friends and colleagues knew she would not be returning in the fall. Ingrid Gray apparently didn't feel she could express what she wanted in the yearbook, so her signature, squeezed beside a lavish poem from the French teacher, was concise and abridged. Did she ever write the long letter? What would it say? Advice to a friend? An apology? An assurance?

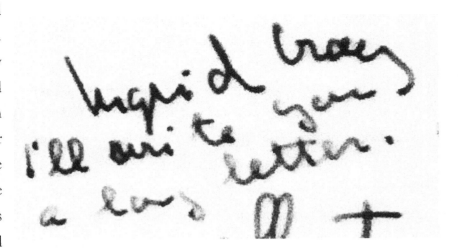

A question?

A wife asked me a question, thirty years later, in 1979. She was married to my practice-teaching mentor. During our "office hours" over the course of our three months together, he'd revealed to me his dissatisfaction with his sex life, that his wife was too inhibited, even that she didn't move her hips. Once he'd taken me to the booths of sex videos in an adult bookstore in a nearby military town. Later, because I lived 40 miles from the school and had an early event the next day, he suggested I stay at his house one night near the end of the semester. Around his kitchen table, it was his idea to roll a joint and share it with me and his wife. Suddenly remembering an evening obligation at school, he abandoned us there together, stoned. Me for the first time.

"Does he ever talk about me at school? … I mean, did he tell you anything … about us, about me, about … I've lost him, haven't I? *Have* I?"

An evocative photo looks out of my grandmother's photo album. It's labeled simply, *Elinore November 1948*. The photos before are summerish, the ones after definitely winter. It is the lone photo of her resume gap. Mom is dressed up, holding her dachshund, and stands facing the camera, posing for the photo. It's an event, a documentation, a milestone. Mom is returning to Chadwick school. Before November 1948 was over, she was back in California, taking a photo of a young man holding her dog.

The reasons Mom returned to her job will remain more mysterious than whatever form of harassment she experienced and by whom. She may have talked to the headmistress Mrs. Chadwick or to a friend (like Ingrid whose husband could have been completely *un*involved in the drama). She would have had to tell her mother something about why she was not returning to work in the fall. Some pressure to resume to her career might have come from both coasts. Mom was back in her girlhood bedroom indefinitely, without a job. And Chadwick School had not filled Mom's position by the time they printed a brochure that listed the '48-49 faculty, including newly hired Ed Babbott.

Mrs. Chadwick's inscription in Mom's 1948 yearbook is almost as evocative as the photo of a young woman dressed for travel in November of that same year.

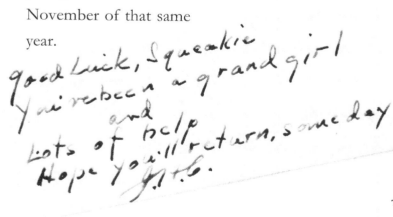

good Luck, Squeakie
You've been a grand girl
and
Lots of help
Hope you'll return, some day
M.C.

CHADWICK
SCHOOL

BULLETIN OF INFORMATION
1948-1949

TEACHING PERSONNEL

Babbott, Edward, A. B. M. A. Swarthmore College Stanford University	English, History
To Be Appointed	Girls' Physical Education

151

She's been a girl, grand and helpful. The door is left open for Mom to change her mind.

It's logical to assume one wouldn't say "hope you return" to an employee resigning to take a new job or to get married in another state. It's something that might be said if an employee leaves to join the military, to go back to school, to raise a family, to care for elderly parents—life choices that have a finite time-length—*or* if an employee has had a bad experience from which she seeks escape. So Mrs. Chadwick's yearbook epilogue suggests she was told something of why Mom was leaving. If the man's expression of interest in Mom reached the levels of frequent phone calls, suggestions for meetings, or groping, would Mrs. Chadwick have let Mom go without also reacting vis-à-vis the man? Yet if the man was not an employee, what choice would the headmistress have?

Chadwick School paid its faculty well below the already poor pay grade of public school teachers. Add that fact to the post-war population surge which caused record need for a new supply of teachers, and experienced teachers saw an open path to career improvement. This apparently wasn't true for Mom (having no academic subject), but it may have been the case for Ingrid Gray. The 1949 faculty directory gave a San Pedro address for Ingrid Gray. In 1953 - 58 the San Pedro newspaper carried various articles about a public school which included a kindergarten teacher named Ingrid Gray. Did Mrs. Chadwick encourage Ingrid to pursue a better-paying job? Or was she just aware that Ingrid might be leaning that direction? Did Mrs. Chadwick know that Ray and Irma Jahn planned an extended stay in Europe during the next academic year? Is that how she reassured Mom that she could come back to work at Chadwick School, forecasting a broad faculty sea-change starting in fall 1949? Auspiciously, the same date Ralph Mazza, who'd graduated in Chadwick's first class, would be ready to begin teaching chemistry after WWII and GI-Bill college.

Or did she simply gaslight Mom with *You were imagining it*?

As to what Mom's mother might have said, that's easy because she wrote it—with quotes acknowledging its timelessness, and its cliché—in Mom's 1942 high school yearbook.

There are only these facts: Both Ray Jahn and Ingrid Gray were still on faculty in 1948-49. And both were gone in fall 1949 when Mom met the

"*Keep your chin up*"
Mother

181

152

new chemistry teacher. Her truncated school year of 1948-49—her near resume gap—might have been the most crucial in the development of Mom's independence. It might have made her someone I should have talked to when I twice stepped away from facing life, both times precipitated by a man's "flirting."

Yearbook Matchmaker

She sat in the upholstered rocking chair where she had nursed all five of us. There was no room for us to share the rocker now. We hovered over the back or kneeled beside the arms. She was flipping through a yearbook. It was probably one of my two elder sisters' yearbooks, at a time when having any high school yearbook in the house was still new. Of course she looked at the group photos featuring her daughter(s), the band and orchestra, the honor roll. Then on to the class photos. She flipped through the pages, her fingers tracing the rows of thumbnail images as though reading braille. Then she stopped. "Oh," she declared, "he's cute, why don't you go with him?"

My sisters, only a year apart in school, immediately bent over the open yearbook to see who had elicited such a statement from Mom. But the layers of preposterousness—that *we* could choose who to "go with," and do it based only on a yearbook photo—overtook any retained memory of who that special boy might be.

Imagining, or even manipulating, one's children's "mates" doesn't need psychological probing. Parents might look forward to it with excitement … or dread. And children doing the conceiving or even maneuvering new mates for a parent made single in midlife is stuff for romcom or sitcom plots. (So probably is unexceptional?) But our parents never became single, so all envisioning of other partners for them is limited to their love-lives before each other. I think there are two reasons children might do this: we either want to assume our parents never looked at anyone else, or that of course they did. Both motives tinged with existential anxiety over the fragile chain of events that led to our existence. What if they *had* met and loved someone else first?

There were no stories told of former boyfriends or girlfriends from either Mom or Dad. For some reason, for decades, this translated into assuming both of them had never tested romance before each other.

The assumption that Mom never had a boyfriend before Dad turned into a question after her death when, with the help of a sister, I archived Mom's paper keepsakes: Pre-1950 photo albums, letters, news clippings, brochures, and a dozen yearbooks, starting her freshman year of high school through her first four years of teaching. It is the latter group, the yearbooks, that might let me ask her—as she asked me once, after she and Dad chaperoned a trip to the mountains with my two girlfriends and three boys—"Which one do you like?"

> For Dad, this may have been true. In the army, in the officers' quarters in Nuremberg—a conscripted private house—he kept his cousin's photo on his bureau so his German housekeeper would assume he had a girlfriend or wife and she wouldn't try to instigate an occupation-romance. He told a story (and didn't tell it until he was 97 years old) about having a female friend in college after the war who borrowed the Leica camera he'd bought in Nuremberg. "Not a girlfriend," he said. *Would she have liked to be?* "I don't know," he said. Hypothesis: He never tried. Because: His covenant with the Catholic Church. I only knew Dad as a lapsed Catholic. When I was 8 or 10, I asked him why he didn't go to Sunday school with us, and he said "because I've already learned everything." I never asked again, but much later he told my sister-in-law that in his 20s one or two young women "offered themselves" to him, and, despite the temptation, he declined because of the Church's insistence that sex not happen until marriage. One of those young ladies asked him if he even liked women. But, he told my sister-in-law, when he met Mom he knew he would do whatever she wanted. Apparently instead of "offering herself," what she wanted was to be married first as well. He also told my sister-in-law that before he met Mom, he left the Church because it didn't seem right that the Church wanted him to feel so frustrated all the time. He likely did not use the word *frustrated*.

Attractive (adj, from the verb *attract,* to cause to approach or adhere)

In 1938 (and many years after that) yearbooks only printed group photos of freshman, sophomore and junior classes. It also appears the custom of signing a special friend's yearbook with a whole page of handwritten sentiment, or even signing with several lines of sentiment, had yet to be established. They just signed their names. But there's still a little to chew on in the 1942 Newtonian yearbook, Mom's senior year.

Other than the page dedicated to the students who were not completing their schooling because they'd enlisted in the armed forces (and the school had yet to encounter a war death), it's not very evident the country was six months into a global conflict. The list of "statistics" gleaned from a survey of the huge high school's student body—with a senior class numbering over 750—look like someone's clichéd invention to depict teenagers in 1942. But it seems they were who we think they were.

GENERAL STATISTICS

Favorite Orchestra — GLENN MILLER
Favorite Newspaper — GLOBE
Favorite Magazine — LIFE
Favorite Sport — FOOTBALL
Favorite Subject — ENGLISH
Favorite Men's College — HARVARD
Favorite Women's College — WELLESLEY
Favorite Fiction — GONE WITH THE WIND
Favorite Non-Fiction — BERLIN DIARY
Favorite Actor — GARY COOPER
Favorite Actress — BETTE DAVIS
Most Admired Man — PRESIDENT ROOSEVELT
Most Admired Woman — MRS. ROOSEVELT

Among the school's groups are social studies, mathematics, science and literature clubs; aviation club; outing club (one for girls, one for boys, and it meant trips, not revealing personal information); personality club (girls only); National Honor Society, and every expected sport, including field hockey and lacrosse. Awards were for (boy and girl of each): Most athletic, most popular, best looking, most versatile, friendliest, most likely to succeed, best informed, best sense of humor, and most original. Mom was runner-up for most athletic. Most of the academic and social clubs were given one page, but there's a two-page spread for "The Ten Most Beautiful Girls" (no parallel spread for boys). Here the ten girls have their senior

photo a second time in the yearbook, much bigger than in the class list. Who voted for these girls, and what made them beautiful? Their hairstyles, their expressions, their skin and lips—all as universal as the list of *favorites*. Were they assumed to be most beautiful because they got the most attention from boys, had steady boyfriends, or many boyfriends? Was this why Mom was not among them? Were they—am *I*— conflating beauty with the potential for at least a romance even if not a more profound relationship? (Consider the real meaning of the word *attractive*.)

Didn't Mom (jokingly) choose what boys my sister should "go with" by virtue of their cuteness? Isn't that the nature of modern-era American adolescence? As much as the drawing the 1942 yearbook staff chose to come before the class photo pages is emblematic of … well, a lot. (That's a stack of *books* he's carrying. Are half hers, or does she just not have books?)

After a decade in which cream eye shadow and pencil-thin eyebrows were featured traits, the top make-up trait of the 40s was an overwhelming preference for red, redder and reddest lips[1], without as much attention to the eyebrows. Face powder remained in vogue (note drawing), but liquid mascara was yet to be invented.

[1] https://glamourdaze.com/history-of-makeup/1940s

While Mom did dress up for her senior photo, the airbrushed portrait can't be evidence of any preoccupation (or lack thereof) with make-up. My earliest memories of my mother's appearance feature the bright, dark red lipstick. But no other make-up. There was no pancake, no blush, no eyeshadow or mascara in her bathroom or on her dresser. And when her daughters started junior high, no introduction to anything but deodorant. Likewise when we entered high school, if the topic of make-up were to come up, it would have to have come from us. I doubt it did. I was asking for 501 Levi's and desert boots and never considered an appeal for Maybelline or Cover Girl. But it might be self-deception to suppose that Mom didn't want the bother of make-up between swimming, basketball and field hockey. Does the team photo of the tennis team show Mom (lower right) ostensibly without her lipstick, or has hers worn off and the notion of reapplying just wasn't the first thing on her mind? Am I

trying to overlay my own androgyny and (resultant?) scant interest from boys onto her? Yes, I must be, because the field hockey team photo makes all the athletes' lipstick look like it was applied directly to the photo, and Mom's eyes (lower left) are vividly, dramatically, shadowy.

Probably the best representation of Mom's attitude toward female beauty, or how much a girl should *try* in order to get male attention (as well as the supremacy of lipstick in makeup priority), is in a 1945 cartoon she kept with her saved clippings and scrapbook items, possibly sent to her by *her* mother (it's the kind of thing Mom did with us, although that habit could also mean she clipped this one for herself).

"Don't object to a little lipstick, Henry! A girl her age always wants to look her best!"

Regardless of how *cute* she was, the high school yearbooks offer nothing toward whether or not she dated, went-around with anyone, hooked-up, had a steady, or any of the other euphemisms throughout the decades.

159

He's Cute, Mom, Did You Want to Go With Him?

Mom's college yearbooks are not useful: it was Sergeant College of Physical Education *for Women*. For four years, Mom savored the camaraderie and solidarity of an all-female community-living arrangement. Besides, men were scarce between 1942 and 1946. Mom said

she wasn't interested in the "90-day-wonders" attending officers' training at nearby Harvard. What mom learned to love, instead of a man, was living among those with whom you worked and played. Six decades later she actually dreamed of moving to a continuing-care retirement community. Her first job teaching physical education at a private boarding school in California allowed the community-living quality of college to continue, although it was, compared to her dorm-and-campus in Cambridge, more isolated.

On the yet-to-be developed Palos Verdes Peninsula, just west of Long Beach, California, Chadwick Seaside School, which began in a private home in 1936, established its campus in 1938. In 1946, when Mom began work there, the number of faculty for the K-12

academy had grown to 23. At that time, married faculty members did not live on campus, but most of the unmarried teachers did live in provided housing and ate in the school's dining hall where faculty presided over "family style" dinner tables of mixed-aged students. In her photo album commemorating her first year, she only photographed campus events, athletic team sports, plus one local carnival.

Mom was young, pretty, athletic, gregarious and adventurous, but not reckless or immodest … what friendships with young men did she make? What I'm looking for in her first-year album are any photos she took of young men, labeled with their names. This would indicate her interest (if my photos of 6th grade camp are any proof). There are a few, the most provocative being a local tennis semi-pro. But he was married and was no longer a coach at Chadwick the following year, 1947-48. *That* was the year, her second in the job, when Mom experienced unwanted attention from the husband of a friend, which led her to resign in June. Despite my conjectures in the previous essay, "#MomToo," I don't know anything specific about the (not yet unlawful) sexual harassment she may have encountered, nor how she was persuaded to resume her job.

When I was 12, I read a YA novel titled *Special Year*. In it a girl learns to adapt to the social pressures of adolescence, (which included updating her wardrobe—what a terrible book it was). But the title has stuck; perhaps a yearning to think I could have had a *special year*. I'm going to assert that Mom did have one, except not a year of conforming to popular styles and behavior, but one of forming an identity, a will, and principles through autonomy *after almost giving up and going home*, even if she was not attempting complete self-sufficiency.

So Mom returned (late) for the 1948-49 school year. And as soon as she returned in November, bringing her dachshund with her from Massachusetts, she took a photo of a young

man, seated outside the faculty rooms, embracing her dog.

He *is* cute. Could this have been the one?

Would you have taken him instead of Dad?

No, I won't go there, and I don't have to. There wouldn't have been a choice. Ed Babbott didn't stay in California, and possibly never intended to—the faculty residences listed in the yearbook give his in New Jersey, and the seniors' epigraph of gratitude for "Uncle Ed" noted, with more than a little prophecy, he "thinks the grass is greener in New Jersey." This alone could have made him invincible to any partiality Mom may have shown.

Babbott, Edward French
English, History, Counselor

Ed Babbott came to Chadwick School in 1947 after his degree from Swarthmore and M.A. from Stanford. In his 2nd year at Chadwick, counseling was added to his duties as an English teacher. Although he had registered for the draft in 1942, he did not serve in the military. In 1948 his California voter registration gave his residence as Chadwick School. In April 1949 he posted a want ad for a camera in a local newspaper. After the '48-49

WANTED
WANTED, Kodak Retina, 1 with coated 3.5 Ektar lens. Babbott Chadwick. Rolling Hills, Lomita.

school year ended, Ed and his newly acquired camera were on a passenger ship for Southampton, England; his address on the manifest was given as Connecticut. The manifest said he intended to be abroad two months, but he stayed and taught for a year in Switzerland. He returned to the U.S. in August 1950; in June 1951 a news brief in a Pennsylvania newspaper reported that Ed Babbott was chaperoning students from The George School on a summer work project in a Martinshof, Germany refugee settlement. The news item summarized Babbott's young career, his undergrad at Swarthmore, grad school at Stanford, and teaching abroad, but not the two years at Chadwick. Was it the reporter or Ed who decided on the omission? Archived yearbooks

show Babbott still teaching at The George School through June 1955. When his engagement was announced in November 1955, he was teaching at a high school in New Jersey while working on his PhD at NYU. He was married the following February. He became a guidance counselor at the New Jersey high school in 1961, and in 1964, with a "Dr." in front of his name, he was the school's guidance director. During the 1960s, Ed was part of a grassroots conservation movement to save New Jersey swampland. That committee evolved into the New Jersey Conservation Foundation, for which Ed served as a trustee for more than 40 years. His daughter, five years younger than me, is a psychologist and poet. Still a photographer, Ed and his daughter co-authored a book of poetry and photographs, *Into the Great Swamp*. It was published in 2015, the year of my mother's death.

The Things We Do For Love

Before mixtapes, there were ways to express our sentimental interest in someone else. Mine was a wall-hanging of an embroidered poem.

> ... Was there ever a high school mash note as intimate as a mixtape? ... Of course, these curated cassettes were more than just calling cards -- they also expressed complex feelings about the recipient.
>
> "Love's Mixtapes Lost: The High School Cassettes We Can't Throw Away" by Jennifer Maertz, 2015, KQED

True, the recipient never laughed, but he also rarely answered, probably didn't know how to listen, and *never* reassured. He did once say "will you go steady with me?" plaintive and vulnerable, and I didn't exactly answer *that*. Maybe we were even. Until he started playing "can you get out of this one" on the bench seat of his van when he took me home from school—the only place he ever "took" me. The embroidered poem was a gift for this boy's 16th birthday; he had a July birthday and someone was hosting a party. I sat at home stitching my gift every June afternoon after summer school. He opened it in front of kids we both knew. He looked at me momentously with his dark sensitive eyes (which I later determined to actually be rather opaque). Because I remember all this, I can also place the gift to be prior to our future skirmishes in his van.

Besides the inappropriateness (or extreme irony) of the wall-hanging's message and the mystery of the primeval man and bull, the significant thing about my offering is that it is now in *my* possession. About 5 years after the gift was made, no longer any contact between us, a mutual friend who was living at the boy's parents' house told me he had seen the wall-hanging rolled up in the closet, so I asked him to sneak it out for me. He might have been about to get it simply by asking, but, still so young, we opted for a furtive return of my display of ardor. Most don't have any more than a memory of their lost token, for better or worse.

If Mom made a craft for Ed Babbott, (or any another man) certainly it's decomposed in a landfill by now. But I might have the residual evidence.

Firstly, Mom had an artistic—or at least artisan —proclivity. Besides the typical ceramics and watercolor taken up in later life, she'd been the one to draw the (popular in that era) caricatures for each senior in her college yearbook. (←This one is *not* a character of herself.) She'd suggested and

> *When I was in college I worked on a painting for a boy I liked. We had dated a few times. The painting was the head of a woman singer with open mouth and closed eyes. The whole painting, including the woman's head, was broken into random shapes. All the background was done in cool colors and the singer in warm colors. Streaming across the painting was a curvy keyboard, in black and white. The shapes were precisely and cleanly painted with a single color each. It was on a large canvas, at least 2 1/2 feet square, in acrylic paints.*
>
> *I brought it to him one day when we were going to the beach. He thanked me, said it was great of me to do that, and set it against the wall in his room. We went to the beach. The next time I saw him was at a school concert, and he was with another girl.*
>
> — My sister

designed a logo for Chadwick School (the Dolphins). I have an embroidered tablecloth and napkins she made for her mother when she was living single at Chadwick. As a mother, she taught us how to make valentines with lace and hearts that sprang off the surface, and another kind of card with flowers or leaves preserved under wax paper and tissue. Would making a card for a man be off her footpath?

I wouldn't have conjured the possibility if it weren't for the 1949 Chadwick yearbook. Ed Babbott was leaving Chadwick after the spring '49 semester, but yearbooks would have been distributed before the end of the school year so signatures could be gathered. Mom had two copies of the '49 yearbook, one with all the inscriptions she'd gathered (mostly from students); the other was blank of signatures. In the unsigned one, she'd cut out the head of a young man. Not the sort of face-cutting-out done in anger when excising a former spouse or boy/girlfriend from a group photo. After all, she left the same photo intact in the copy of the yearbook where she gathered autographs. While it may be a stretch, the cut-out head could have been part of some kind of collage, a goodbye or congratulations card, maybe given from the entire faculty, or maybe not. Probably not … because the blank yearbook has just one other cut-out head: Mom's.

Mom's cut out head is her faculty photo. None of the other faculty photos are disturbed, including Ed Babbott's. If Mom were going to paste the young man's cut-out face with hers on a card, one would assume she'd use his face from his faculty photo if she could—then the photos would be the same size. After cutting out the pictures, she would have been able to cut around the heads and then float them on a different background—something she learned when on the 1946 yearbook staff in college (cutting-edge "photoshopping" technique of the era).

In the maddening style of high school yearbooks—present in Mom's high school and college yearbooks, in the Chadwick yearbooks, persisting through mine and likely continuing to this day—the candid snapshots of campus life are un-captioned. Sometimes mashed together in a messy collage, sometimes barely bigger than a 35mm slide with far too much white space between them, they might have told a story to giggling 17-year-olds bent over an old-fashioned layout table, but as any record of anything, they're near worthless. So the young man whose head Mom cut from the unsigned copy of the '49 yearbook is unidentified. Looking directly at the camera with a daring smile as he takes off his shirt, he may have been challenged to show off the tattoo on his upper arm. At the time tattoos were usually a

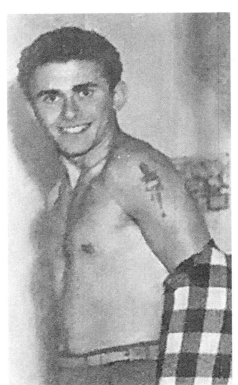

memento of the armed services. The whole context says he is not a student. But nowhere else in the yearbook is there a young adult male who looks remotely similar. Except Ed Babbott. And even that's a stretch. If I had the original photos instead of scans from the yearbook, I could probably determine the unidentified man has hair a different texture, possibly parted on the opposite side. In all

of the photos I found of Ed Babbott except when he was in his 90s, he wore his glasses. Ed's face is long and thin in his Chadwick faculty photo, but not in his Swarthmore class photo from just 5 years previous. It remains possible … but not probable.

Winning Teams

A remaining yearbook hint is, I think, a red herring … or would be if someone created this mystery on purpose in 1949 for me to use as escapism in 2020. A photo of Mom in the *sports* section of the yearbook shows her in her college tunic and a ballcap, holding a softball. In the caption, written by students: *Elinore Young, Constantly on the Go … produces winning teams in every sport … contagious giggle … secret liking for the mailman … always at the right spot at the right time.*

Mom was a letter-writer, to her mother, her sister, her brother, probably to her college friends. It's not difficult to imagine that the daily mail was something she looked forward to. At her age, I was also living alone for the first time. I utterly recall waiting for the sound— *tonk*—of envelopes hitting the bottoms of the mail slots in the foyer of my tenement apartment in Brooklyn. Perhaps Mom had a daily habit of asking, "is the mail here yet?" Maybe

166

even "has the mailman come today?" Too easy for a student to render this into a joke about a crush on the letter carrier, when in reality she was 3,000 miles from home—a home she'd chosen to return to permanently the previous year, only to relent and try again. Was this school in California the right spot at the right time?

Swarthmore alumni ran an obituary for Ed Babbott in 2019: … *Ed was a magician of the highest order. … His magic was infectious, making cups half-full to overflowing; transforming loneliness to connection; in sum, you left an encounter with Ed feeling as though you genuinely mattered.*

He may have done no more than hold her dog and smile for a photo, but I hope, at least, Ed Babbott worked his magic for her.

In fall 1949, Mom's 4th year, there was a new chemistry teacher. An alumni of Chadwick's first graduating class and the first scholarship student, he'd returned from war-interrupted college, occupied Nuremberg, then a resumption of college. In his first semester teaching at Chadwick, he assisted a student with an eye injury—the nature of the assistance and injury are beyond artifactual research, but the boy, from the family of a real estate mogul and arts philanthropist, himself became a famous benefactor. Dr. Peter Bing MD donated $50 million to Stanford University to build a world-class concert hall.

In 1949, Peter's mother acknowledged Dad's assistance to her son with 2 tickets to a Vladimir Horowitz concert. Newly back in town, Dad couldn't find a friend to use the second ticket, so he asked the girls' P.E. teacher. At the end of the evening, she kissed him. Otherwise, he said, it might have ended there. Because, despite his immediate infatuation with her, any move toward anything more would have to come from her. Fortunately (for myself and my siblings), whatever she had experienced two years before that almost led her to quit and go home, Mom did not step back, she leaned in.

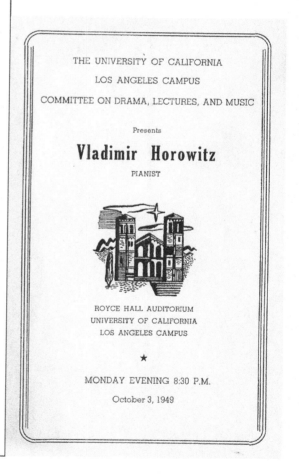

THE UNIVERSITY OF CALIFORNIA
LOS ANGELES CAMPUS

COMMITTEE ON DRAMA, LECTURES, AND MUSIC

Presents

Vladimir Horowitz
PIANIST

ROYCE HALL AUDITORIUM
UNIVERSITY OF CALIFORNIA
LOS ANGELES CAMPUS

★

MONDAY EVENING 8:30 P.M.

October 3, 1949

Unhappy at Parties

Maybe I was the one unhappy at parties… starting around junior high. Any parties—including school dances—where kids paired-up, whether dancing in the cafeteria or playing Twister in a basement under black-lights. All were entered into with anticipation of the personal benefits, then disappointment was swiftly commensurate to hope.

Admittedly, the level of letdown—dances where I was never asked to dance, parties where I sat alone on a sofa eating from a bag of stale chips torn open on a coffee table—can be blamed on myself, how I waited to be talked to, waited to be asked, and insisted androgyny should be (just as) appealing because it made me feel not only more myself, but safe.

But parties also included family gatherings. Around the time my age entered double-digits, family events were equally dispiriting. Like when I had to sit in an audience of older aunts and uncles while my sister's violin-playing was showcased. It was reasonably obvious there was a "talented one" among the five Mazza siblings. And it was not me.

My overactive adult awareness of isolation at parties wasn't only due to my own party-malfunctions—those largely caused by who I was and not an indifferent host—and probably began at one particular family wedding-reception. These functions were almost never in a catered banquet hall, but in one of the family's houses with Italian gourmet potluck. At the noteworthy reception in my memory, Mom's coffee table was heaped with wedding gifts—no

registry, the gifts were practical kitchenware and linens, chosen by the giver. In the clutter of mismatched chairs brought to the living room for the occasion, Nana, my paternal grandmother, had been shown to Mom's upholstered rocking chair, which, as always, lured her grandchildren and great-grandchildren to cluster on and around her. And there she stayed.

Somehow, after the party was over, when the guests were thinning, someone came to realize that Nana had stayed in the rocking chair for hours with only a bowl of potato chips to eat; she hadn't gotten a potluck plate with any of the salami, prosciutto, cheese, stuffed mushrooms, fried artichoke, eggplant parmesan, or wedding cake. She was hungry.

I'm sure I was informed of this afterward. I have no memory image of food from the banquet finally being plated and brought to her when Mom realized the oversight. Only the silent horror of what she may have felt being left out of the feast, and that I hadn't made sure Nana was taken care of at ... yes, *my* wedding reception. Perhaps this guilt is a perverse reason that I saved as new—never used, now over 40 years —the hand towels Nana had picked out for me. When my aunt had brought Nana shopping to buy a wedding present, Nana had broken from my color limitation (dark blue) and chose complementary colors. Did I put them carefully away, to sustain their brightness, because I didn't deserve them? Or because I sought to preserve the evidence of Nana's desire for my life to have color.

Mom was the one frankly happy at parties. One time the extended family was expected for a holiday dinner. She and I worked through the morning with cooking and table-setting. My sisters were already married and would be arriving later, as would the other guests. Everyone brought food, so it wasn't up to us to crank out a five-course meal alone. Then the first guest arrived. We could hear the car doors slam, my father's voice out in the driveway, and Mom said, "They're early; I haven't had a chance to change." She'd intended to wear a fancy skirt and fresh blouse, accessorized with some kind of holiday-themed broach. Why did I even know this? I know why I remember: the guests swept into the house arousing the usual shrieks of greetings, and Mom never made it to her bedroom to change. Nor, I don't believe, did she think of it again. She rode the wave of family-gathering crescendo with her usual untempered exhilaration. But *I* couldn't stop imagining the disappointment she must be—*had* to be—hiding, for the holiday outfit she never wore. She even had a food stain on the knit shell top she'd put on to work in the kitchen that morning. She wore it for hours, all through the carnival of feasting, resounding conversation and screeched laughter. Instead of appreciating her resilience, I couldn't look at her, at that smear on her shirt, without the sorrow and compassion—not shame—she apparently didn't even need.

Mom returned to unfettered joy at parties even when she was relegated to a hospital bed in the bedroom I'd once shared with my sisters. The Southern California extended family, my father's side—the next generation aficionados of cooking, hugging, exclaiming, and laughing—gathered to see her. They may have thought of it as a goodbye visit, but she did not. Congestive heart failure had made it near impossible for her to stay conscious in an upright position, she needed round-the-clock nursing assistance; she'd spent the last 15 years of her life with stroke-induced aphasia, re-learning how to process language, which all unraveled when the heart disease took over. But the ecstasy at greeting and being surrounded-by guests who'd gathered to see her was entirely intact. Whenever and in whatever ways I feel myself "becoming my mother," it is never in that way.

I say she *returned* to riding this delight because there were a few occurrences in the years just prior to becoming bedridden when it seemed she did not or could not.

The before-and-after was partitioned by her brain attack. This seems a more apt labelling, since her stroke affected nothing except her brain, and of that nothing except one of the conscious brain's biggest functions, the processing of language. Her mouth and tongue and throat had no trouble forming words; they regularly were the wrong words. In addition, incoming language had to be slowed down, way down, and necessary repetition established her habitual response for the last 15 years of her life, "I understand." However, two people speaking at once—and by obvious extension a family dinner conversation, relatives milling in a living room, or a party in a banquet hall—initiated another response: an imaginary

171

soundproof bubble of retreat. Parties, dinners, girl scout alumni meetings: all shut her out. The only exception: bridge groups, where concentration on numbers and strategy was a different, and unscathed, part of her brain. She could plan and make the refreshments, create the bridge tallies with images of her paintings as covers, then at the gathering she could serve the dessert, play her cards, and briefly lament or affirm her play; if she caught anything else of interest being said, it was a bonus.

The first party after her brain attack was too soon to show her that parties could indefinitely be altered. The brain attack was the day after bypass surgery. Six weeks later when she was sent home from rehab, she was still recovering from the physical punishment of having her heart stopped and restarted, being intubated, and losing a vein in one leg. Compounded by language being a muddle, coming in and going out. But it was Christmas; her five children had gathered from points across the country, so she was, for the first time in weeks, as close to her usual happy as her weakened condition would allow. I was the last to arrive, Christmas night around 9 p.m. By then she'd practiced a line, spoken slowly in a voice hoarsened by the ventilator tube, "Thank you for going to be me."

The character of her aphasia lit up like luminal: opposites and rhymes. ...*for coming* to *see me*. And yet, aren't we all going forward in life to partially become our parents?

Another, much bigger party came six months later. An event none of our weddings, even hers, had been: A banquet-hall gathering of relatives and friends for Mom and Dad's 50th anniversary. Her physical health had resumed, enough for her to climb the steps to the top of Cape Hatteras Light, swim in the waters below the light at night, fish, go clamming, and drive a jet ski.

With so many people attending the anniversary party, I didn't try to stay close to Mom and see how she was handling the atmosphere of greeting, laughing, joking, and reminiscing that used to be a milieu she treasured. In another unusual move, an event photographer / videographer was hired and we all, even Mom, left our cameras home. Perhaps any photo showing Mom anything but radiant,

172

or at least pleased, was left out of the photographer's portfolio. But possibly no such photos existed. The party was for her, *about* her; no language barrier prevented her from feeling included and involved. Smiles, hugs, exclamations of greeting—comprehending a conservation was not required.

Similar to the memorial service we would plan in 15 years, the 50th anniversary celebration included a presentation. There was, of course, my sister's violin; my other siblings and a few cousins offered anecdotal stories, and I did a reading from one of the few pieces I had, at the time, that featured my parents. The violin music might have been the only part of the performance Mom "understood" while it was happening. Her eyes were keen and bright; she smiled and clapped and probably laughed whenever Dad did. This party was before she'd adopted certain hand gestures (thumbs-up and, strangely, a peace sign), but after she'd learned to fake cognizance when she had to. The program, plus the party's dancing and some general dinner shots, were included in the professional photographer's video. And, it turned out, that was how Mom was able to fully revel in the party orchestrated for her and Dad. She watched that video over and over, each time putting together or catching something she hadn't grasped before. She even once watched it in another room during another family gathering, when she'd withdrawn to her bubble, away from the havoc of children and grandchildren that continued without her.

The gathering when she re-watched the anniversary-party video was a California post-Christmas dinner, part ham roasted indoors, part tri-tip on the grill on the patio, plus the buffet of familiar Mazza side dishes, from eggplant parmesan to persimmon salad. We'd long since abandoned the childhood tradition of everyone being seated before the food was brought to the table, then Dad serving each plate and passing it around. The tables weren't big enough to hold all the food, people couldn't be herded to take their seats, too many different diet restrictions and preferences. But it seemed to work to have everyone fill their own plates then

find a seat at a pre-set table. Mom and Dad fixed their plates first, choosing the ham, and someone helped Mom carry her plate to the dining room table. I followed them, and sat beside Mom. By habit, from the years of each person being served one at a time, we paused, not eating, to await others with their dinner plates. But almost everyone else had congregated on the patio where the grill was, and when they began to fill plates and eat, they sat at picnic tables out there.

The three of us sat on one side of the table, like the only ones at the adult-table on Thanksgiving, the clamor of the other conversations far removed, outside. Dad had finished pouring wine for himself and Mom. He held his glass in one hand, but didn't lift it from the table. His other hand rested beside his plate. He said, "Where is everybody?"

Did he feel abandoned, left out?

Like the holiday when Mom wore a stained shirt through the whole festivity—if they didn't feel it, I felt it for them.

I left the table and went out to the patio. "Hey, Mom and Dad are sitting alone in here. Can't someone come in and eat with them?"

Eventually the table filled. Especially when the honeycakes (a form of struffoli) were brought out.

The brain attack had permanently eradicated television or movies from Mom's life; dialogue went too quickly for her to follow a story, and there was no rewinding of TV shows to hear something again (as I am the beneficiary of now). Reading was slower than before, but she wanted it so badly, she grabbed and held fast to keep the ability from deserting her. What remained *un*impaired: cooking, painting watercolors, crocheting, and—except when it came to explaining the game rules to someone else—playing cards. She had cards and mahjong on her computer, then my brother gave her an iPad with all her games loaded. I'm not sure she ever used the tablet for email or the internet—she'd learned some basic computer tasks following the brain attack, but usually had to follow step-by-step instructions which several of us wrote and printed for her. But that iPad, left plugged in on a sofa, became her companion in the isolation bubble. As Dad continued to watch a movie or the news in the den, Mom would leave her recliner in front of the TV, slip around the corner to her loveseat in the front room and pull the iPad from under a cushion for solitaire, hearts, even bridge. The device wasn't referred to as an iPad or tablet or even computer, but *Mom's games*.

For years, most family gatherings had consolidated into playing a game. (A useful trait in any family divided by politics.) Later, the other, more recent, family-visit scaffold: doing a jigsaw puzzle. I was surprised when the 2020 pandemic created a run on puzzles; I'd thought them too archaic and laborious, the end accomplishment not heady enough, for most families now. But long before 2020, puzzles had become an invaluable way to spend

time together and to interact with Mom at her house.

Card games and puzzles, however, were seldom in use at other people's houses: My siblings, their children, their partners and spouses were a new generation of the chaos of conversation, animated voices, interruptions, and shouted laughter that had been the atmosphere at my grandfather's house. Plus a more recent addition of absorbed debates between PhDs in chemistry, geology, neuroscience, and music, who might be discussing anything from astronomy to public education to favorite films. At some point, Mom began bringing her iPad to these gatherings, and she removed herself to another room to recognize her world, her own consciousness, over a hand of solitaire.

"Mom's gone," one of us would say. The exact words my father used when he called to tell me she'd died.

When congestive heart failure forced Mom to a hospice bed in 2014, and her decade-ago speech-therapy language improvement waned from lack of oxygen … music, again, seemed an obvious way to communicate, putting my sister's violin-playing back in its place centerstage at family gatherings. We didn't pause to wonder *what* was being communicated. That my sister was a professional violinist was an obvious source of pride for our parents. Would Mom listen with a modicum of *self*-pride as well, that she had been the bedrock of encouragement (and mandate) that had secured my sister's practicing habits? Perhaps additional pride that some friends or family were present to notice her daughter's accomplishment as well? While I may have had momentary flashbacks to those long-ago family gatherings when my sister was shown off to grandparents and aunts, I think what we hoped for in the hospice-bedroom concerts was the comfort of Mom being able to hear and understand at least one of her children.

Unlike at a memorial program, it would have been preposterous to offer to read to Mom, and I never even considered it. My books had "caught up" with the violin as far as parental esteem, but were far more difficult to share with friends, relatives, or parents. Books that didn't adhere to popular expectations, especially when they didn't "make a million" or result in appearances on talk shows are difficult for some people to "measure." But the sublime sound of an accomplished solo violin, and employment in a symphony orchestra are tangible attainment.

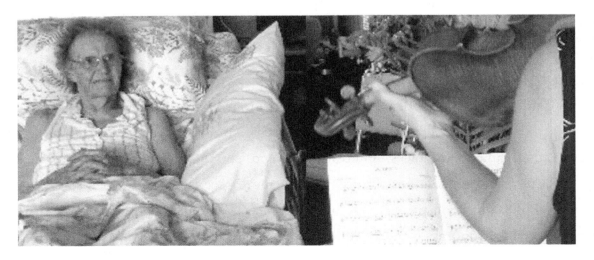

And then … while the sheet music was being shuffled between tunes, Mom grasped my arm, tugged me closer, and whispered with breathless hoarseness, "No … more … music."

What did *I* say? What *could* I say?

It's almost time for dinner …?

The guests want to hear it … ?

It'll be over soon … ?

No one else heard her, and I didn't tell anyone what she'd said … until now. I'm glad I waited; it's taken until now to understand: She wasn't saying she disliked the sometimes silky, always vivid, occasionally brash tone of the violin playing familiar folk melodies or light classical, or that she no longer wanted to hear her daughter's talent displayed. I think her desire for it to end had to do with what she needed *more*. For the people in the room to look at *her*, smile at her, talk to her, even if she didn't follow everything they said. The damaged half of her brain craved a comfort that the healthy half couldn't give.

> Instrumental music is decoded in the brain on the opposite side from the language centers. But researchers have discovered songs – with lyrics – engage both sides of the brain simultaneously and differently than when either language or music is perceived alone. From this discovery researchers plan to learn how the brain combines the two streams of information into a coherent experience.
>
> Dr. Robert Zatorre, McGill University's Montreal Neurological Institute, and Dr Daniela Sammer, Max Planck Institute for Cognition, and Neurosciences https://n.pr/2HHsvCx
>
> In the first weeks after her brain attack, Mom **was singing Christmas songs, all the words intact.**

Mom's last party was another holiday season. For many of us, December was the best month for travel, yet the traditions of other seasonal holidays—which Mom had always planned with zeal—continued to buoy her in the 18 months she spent in a hospice bed. Perhaps feeling anticipation was a form of hope, that same elemental sensation that had carried me into adolescent parties. Until, on arriving, it flamed out.

Just before Christmas, in the first six months of hospice, insurance allowed for a specialized wheelchair. Mom's mind still assumed she would someday get out of this bed (and I expect disapproval that we chose not to tell her otherwise). But Mom's body could not support itself, could barely assist someone else trying to support it, and had difficultly staying conscious if in an upright position. This chair allowed her to lie almost flat, with brief periods

of semi-vertical sitting up. So, to her, the chair was liberation, even optimism. She might have been lifted into it (requiring two men) only a handful of times before the effective time for its use had passed. But the holidays were during that window.

So this would not be a party where an elderly lady would be left in one place and forgotten. When she had to return to bed, the party went with her. A caroling concert, some traditional Christmas eve games, making a showcase

of the shocking silk robe gift from Dad, poring over a book my sister had commercially printed of Mom's best watercolors, then a feast featuring cracked crab, stuffed mushrooms, lasagna, feta salad, homemade cookies, plus tangerines, persimmons, pomegranates and dried figs from Dad's trees.

How much did she know she was the center of concern, the source of wringing emotion, of conflicted aching throats and pulsing adrenalin? Being the center of *anxious*

attention wouldn't be a source of bliss, but belonging, being connected would be. Her world may have shrunk to only these rooms, only a few hours a day, only these people, but she wasn't—had never been—alone.

Apparently, I'm discovering, after all, that Mom was never unhappy at parties.

Us: Serving her, watching her, smiling at her, assisting her, admiring her … and desperately taking photo after photo. To preserve just the moment? For fear we wouldn't remember her upside-down smile?

Maybe more an attempt to make her pleasure eternal.

CRIS MAZZA, one of the originators of the term chick-lit before it meant urban-girls-looking-for-love, is a novelist and memoirist with 20 published books. Her titles include, most recently, a novel, *Yet to Come*, a story of marital angst in California's Imperial County; and *Something Wrong With Her*, a real-time memoir. Mazza's first novel *How to Leave a Country* won the PEN/Nelson Algren Award for book-length fiction. She is also author of the critically acclaimed *Is It Sexual Harassment Yet?* Mazza is a native of Southern California and is a professor in and director of the Program for Writers at the University of Illinois at Chicago.